It Takes All Types!

By Alan W. Brownsword

It Takes All Types!

published by

Baytree Publication Company

for

HRM Press, Inc
P.O. Box 454
San Anselmo, CA 94979

(415) 453-4971

Alan W. Brownsword is founding principal of Performance & Leadership Development, a management consulting and leadership development business based in Washington, D.C. He first encountered the world of psychological type in 1971, trained with Isabel Briggs Myers and David Keirsey and has used type and temperament in his professional consulting career ever since.

Alan's professional interests include team building, leadership and management development. He is internationally recognized for his work in applying type and temperament to managerial behavior.

Before founding P&L, Alan was a professional historian, university educator and director of organization development at the U.S. Office of Education.

Alan is a graduate of Brown University and holds a Ph.D. from the University of Wisconsin.

To My Family: A Study In Type

My Father
Walter Brownsword
1906-1981
INFJ

My Mother
Alma Y. Brownsword
ENTP

My Wife
Joanne J. Brownsword
ESFJ

My Children
Thomas A. Brownsword
ENTP

Susan K. Brownsword
ISFP

Andrew Y. Brownsword
ENTJ

Acknowledgements

Richard S. Goldstein (INFJ)

In 1981, Rick and I set out to write this book. It was going to be a brief introduction to type and temperament. To learn about type, one had to turn to Isabel Briggs Myers' work. To learn about temperament, one turned to David Keirsey. Nowhere was there one book that combined both. We set out to write that book. Our project grew in scope, and Rick's life took him off to other pursuits. He made many contributions in those early days. The title of the book is his, and the first drafts of almost all the descriptions were a result of our collaboration. I regret his not being able to continue. This book is the richer for the contributions he did make.

A. Lad Burgin (ENTJ)

When I began work on this book, I was a career civil servant working for the U.S. Department of Education. Three years ago I became an independent consultant and management trainer. It was Lad who made that transition possible. There is no way I can ever thank him enough for that. His knowledge of type has enriched the content of this book, and without his insistence that I complete it who knows when it would have seen the light of day!

Charles B. Gompertz (ENFJ)

Chuck has brought an impressive range of interests and abilities to our work with type. He and I have happily collaborated in many programs over the past three years. He volunteered to take on the monumental and complex task of shepherding the manuscript through the publication process. For that and so many other things, I am very grateful.

Joanne J. Brownsword (ESFJ)

In addition to everything else, my wife has made two very concrete and invaluable contributions to this book. She has read every sentence—often more than once. When she does not understand what I've written or when she does not like it, she tells me. However impatient and hostile my immediate reaction, I trust her judgment. I know the book will be better if I rewrite those passages. She is also an exceptional proof reader. She is careful, meticulous and disciplined when she sets out to discover errors. There is no one I trust more than her to do the final reading. So, if the book is coherent and relatively error free, thank her. If not, blame my stubbornness and time running out!

L. Alan Feinberg (ENFP)

Alan is an architect, urban planner and artist. His illustration on the front cover shows all kinds of people, doing all kinds of things. He has captured introverts and extraverts of every sort, all together, as we are in life. His drawing reflects the title of the book, *It Takes All Types!*

Graphic Design, Typography and Production by Van Norman/Associates, Fairfax, California.

Table of Contents

Table of Contents

Table of Contents

Introduction

Welcome to the world of psychological type and temperament. It is an exciting world. It gives those who are willing to invest the time to master it some remarkable tools. These tools can give continuing insights into ourselves, others, and situations. They are tools that we can use to identify and make the most effective use of our own strengths. They can help us to recognize and avoid some of our weaknesses. They can help us to understand, appreciate, work, and live more productively and harmoniously with others. They can help us to look at many things and understand what it will take to handle them well. They can help us to more effectively meet life's demands.

The world of psychological type as described in this book began with the work of the pioneering Swiss psychoanalyst, Carl Gustav Jung, who wrote *Pyschological Types* in 1922. It is he who first outlined the basic theory this book is all about. But without the work of two remarkable American women, Katharine C. Briggs and Isabel Briggs Myers, only trained Jungian analysts and their patients would ever have benefitted from Jung's work.

Katharine Briggs read Jung's work soon after it was published in English in 1923. She herself had been developing a theory of psychological type, and she recognized that she and Jung had been thinking in parallel lines. Jung had so clarified what she herself had been thinking that she became an advocate and a promoter of his work.

Undoubtedly, however, her greatest contribution was to interest her daughter Isabel in Jung's theories. Together they added to and enriched Jung's work. Together they embarked on a journey to make his insights available to us all.

For Myers, psychological type became a governing passion of her life. It is to her that we owe the Myers-Briggs Type Indicator, which continues to be the best way for people interested in type to identify that type which describes them best. Her pamphlet, *Introduction to Type*, remains a beautifully written classic. For years it was the only written material available that described Jung's work in simple terms and provided superb, brief descriptions of each of the types. *Gifts Differing*, by Isabel Myers, published after her death in 1980, distills the work of a remarkable life.

As opposed to type, the world of temperament has different historical roots. As far back as the ancient Greeks, observers have seen human behavior as falling into one of four sharply different temperaments. Temperament theory, as it has come to be called, has surfaced, disappeared and resurfaced several times in western civilization. David Keirsey, as a student at Claremont Graduate School shortly after World War II, became intrigued with theories of temperament as described by German scholars in the late nineteenth and early twentieth centuries.

When introduced to the work of Isabel Briggs Myers, he wondered if there was any relationship to the sixteen Jungian types and the four temperaments. There was. Keirsey, therefore, attached temperament theory to the types. He has devoted his scholarly career to developing further temperament theory.

The two approaches, though superficially contradictory, are not. They each provide significant insights into human behavior. To date, there has been no single work that combines the two theories. Myers' work does not attempt to include temperament, and Keirsey rejects critically important parts of Jung's theories.

It is the purpose of this book to introduce readers to both Jung's theories of psychological type as interpreted by Briggs and Myers and to Keirsey's ideas about temperament. The principal focus of this book is on the theories and the descriptions of type and temperament. The first chapter describes the four basic preferences that underlie Jung's work. The second chapter gives detailed descriptions of each type and temperament. The third chapter details Jung's ideas about how the preferences interact to form a whole that is greater than the sum of their parts and addresses briefly how type and temperament theory do not have to be viewed as contradictory.

There is a companion volume that needs to be written. It needs to address more specifically important applications of type and temperament. For knowledge of type and temperament can and has contributed to self insight, to relationships, to parenting, and to education, work, play, and religion. But that comes after learning about the theories themselves! It is for this latter purpose this book was written.

Alan W. Brownsword, Ph.D. (INTP)

Chapter 1

The Preferences

I Introduction

Jung's theory of psychological type deals with three sets of opposites. Katharine C. Briggs and her daughter, Isabel Briggs Myers, added a fourth. The four sets are:

Extraversion and Introversion (E/I) describe two different ways of relating to the world.

> **Extraversion (E)** means focusing one's attention and energy on the world outside self.

> **Introversion (I)** means focusing one's attention and energy on the world inside self.

Sensing and Intuition (S/N) define two ways of collecting and generating information. They deal with the world of **perception.**

> **Sensing (S)** involves the use of the five senses to collect information about specifics. Sensing asks "what are the details?"

> **Intuition (N)** seeks to find meaning, possibilities and relationships in the specifics. Intuition asks "what meaning can I make out of the details?"

Thinking and Feeling (T/F) define two ways of making decisions. They deal with the world of **judgment.**

> **Thinking (T)** uses logic to make decisions. Jung said "thinking links ideas together by logic." Thinking reasons this way: "Given the information I have, what does logic say?"

> **Feeling (F)** uses a valuing process to make decisions. In Jung's definition, feeling "arranges things in accordance with their value." Feeling reasons this way: "Given the information, what do I value?"

Judging and Perceiving (J/P) is the set of opposites that Briggs and Myers added. They describe two different life style orientations and two contrasting ways of relating to the external world.

> **Judging (J)** means relating to the external world in an organized and orderly way. It means making plans and decisions about the external world.

> **Perceiving (P)** means relating to the external world in a flexible and spontaneous way. With regard to the external world, it means collecting information and responding to things as they occur.

Jung's theory of psychological type builds on these sets of opposites in three ways:

1. **Both/And.** We all do extraverted and introverted things. We all use sensing and intuition to collect and generate information. We all make thinking and feeling decisions, and many decisions are a mixture of both processes of reasoning. We all relate to the external world in judging and perceiving ways.

2. **Either/Or.** Each pair of opposites also act as preferences. We all experience a pull to one side of each pair of opposites that is as pervasive as gravity. Hence, we are either

extraverted or introverted types. We prefer either sensing or intuition when we are dealing with the world of perception. We approach decisions with either thinking or feeling. And we prefer to live our outer lives in a judging or a perceiving attitude.

3. **Both/And and Either/Or.** In each of the sixteen types, the preferences and their opposites combine according to specific and prescribed patterns. The fullest appreciation of each type can only come from understanding how the preferences and their opposites combine. For each psychological type, the whole is, indeed, greater than the sum of its parts.

The remainder of this chapter describes the four sets of opposites, emphasizing their both/and and either/or nature.

II Extraversion and Introversion
Extraverts or Introverts

Very few people are aware of it, but Jung created the words "extraversion" and "introversion." He did so to distinguish the two worlds in which all of us live. There is, he suggested, a world outside ourselves, and there is a world inside us. We all live in both worlds, but not simultaneously. In order to focus on the world outside, we shut off our awareness of the world within. In order to listen to our inner dialogue, we turn away from the world outside.

Activities we get involved in can fit under one or the other of these terms. We are extraverting when we:

- speak to someone
- concentrate on what others say
- handle a tool
- look at a picture or painting
- move our fingers over a computer keyboard

We are introverting when we:

- think through inside what we want to say
- restate internally what we think we heard
- pay attention to how we feel
- think about what others think of us
- carry on a conversation with a book

The key distinction is whether the primary focus of one's attention and energy is directed outward or inward. While all of us do extraverted and introverted things, we do not do them all equally well. Extraverts are more at home with extraverted activities. They find introverted things either difficult, boring or both. Extraversion is their "home base;" introversion is a place they visit. Extraverted activities come naturally to them; introverted things do not. Extraverted things give them energy; introverted activities are draining and often require concentration. Anything that involves extraversion involves their "natural" skills. Those things that involve introversion involve "acquired" skills.

With some extraverts, the gravitational pull of extraversion is very strong. These extraverts actively avoid introverted activities. If given no choice, they can become depressed or frustrated. They feel restless, irritable, and moody. For other extraverts, the gravitational pull is not so strong. They can do many introverted things easily and, in fact, may even enjoy doing them. In short, some extraverts have few "acquired" introverted skills, others have many.

With introverts, it is, of course, just the opposite. They are more at home with introverted activities. They find extraverted things draining. Whatever requires introversion they do naturally. Extraverted projects require more effort and planning. Introverts will do extraverted things better if they can prepare internally for them. Extraversion takes concentration and effort.

As with extraverts, introverts differ in the strength of the gravitational pull of introversion. For some, extraverted things are both difficult and painful. Others have well developed extraverted skills. They enjoy doing extraverted things, and sometimes even feel energized doing them. In the end, however, too much extraversion can cause them to feel disoriented.

Appearances can be deceptive. We may do so many extraverted things well that others see us as extraverts. Or we may seem so quiet and reflective that others think of us as introverts. If, however, the natural pull—the first instinct—is to interact with the external world, we are extraverts. We may be extraverts with a well developed introverted side, but we are extraverts. If, on the other hand, our first impulse—our natural inclination—is to pull inside, then we are introverts. Again, we can have many extraverted skills, but we are nonetheless introverts.

Good statistics on the distribution of extraverts and introverts in the general population do not exist. From the evidence we do have, approximately 70% of the population are extraverts, 30% introverts.

As the dialogue and summary chart on the following pages illustrate, our preference for extraversion or introversion, however marked or mild, powerfully affects our behavior.

Extravert: I get a lot of energy from being with others.

Introvert: I am drained when I spend a lot of time with others, particularly when I'm with strangers.

Extravert: I get bored and restless if I spend a lot of time alone.

Introvert: I need time alone to recharge my batteries—to restore my energy.

Extravert: I figure things out best when I can talk things over with others.

Introvert: I need time alone to figure things out, to get in touch with my inner world.

Extravert: I turn to others when I need affirmation, confirmation, or verification.

Introvert: I turn inward when I need affirmation, confirmation, or verification.

Extravert: I am good at meeting people.

Introvert: I have to exert an effort to meet people, and I may avoid or postpone doing so.

Extravert: I have good verbal skills and am good at making conversation.

Introvert: I often find the give-and-take of free-flowing conversation somewhat difficult to keep up with, and I have trouble thinking of the right thing to say on the spur of the moment.

Extravert: I speak up at meetings easily and often.

Introvert: I often hold back at meetings, then have trouble getting into the discussion.

Extravert: I am likely to speak first, think later—and suffer from "foot-in-mouth" problems!

Introvert: I am likely to think afterwards of the thing to say—I suffer from the "why didn't I think to say . . ." syndrome!

Extravert: I dislike or avoid writing.

Introvert: I have good writing skills and often actually prefer presenting my ideas in writing.

Extravert: I tend to be very aware of who or what is around me.

Introvert: I am often not very observant of what's going on in the world around me.

Extravert: I don't usually pay much attention to what's going on inside me.

Introvert: I am introspective—I'm generally very aware of my inner reactions.

Extravert: I am generally easy to get to know. I show the world what I really am—I don't surprise people with "hidden sides" of my personality.

Introvert: I am generally difficult to get to know. I don't very often show the world what I really am—I have important "hidden sides" of my personality and can surprise people who think they know me well!

Common Characteristics of Extraverts	Common Characteristics of Introverts
We are energized when we are with others.	Time alone is important to us.
We can be drained or bored if we spend too much time alone.	Too much time with people, particularly strangers, is often draining.
We seek affirmation, confirmation, or verification of ourselves from others, from the external world.	We seek affirmation, confirmation, or verification from our inner experience, from what goes on inside us.
We figure things out most comfortably when we can talk things over with others.	We need time alone to figure things out, to to get in touch with our introspective strength.
We are good at meeting new people.	We must exert an effort to meet new people; we may avoid or postpone doing so.
We have good verbal skills. We are good at making conversation.	We may find the give-and-take of verbal interaction somewhat difficult to keep up with, may have touble thinking of the right thing to say on the spur of the moment.
At meetings, we speak out easily and often.	At meetings, we may hold back, then have trouble getting into the discussion.
We are likely to speak first, think later—and suffer from "foot-in-mouth" problems!	We are likely to think afterwards of the thing to say—suffer from the "why didn't I think to say . . ." syndrome!
We may dislike or avoid writing.	We often have good writing skills and may actually prefer presenting our ideas in writing.
We tend to be very aware of who or what is around us.	We may not be highly observant of the outer environment.
We may be unaware of what's going on inside us.	We tend to be introspective—very aware of our inner reactions.
We are generally easy to get to know.	We are generally difficult to get to know.
We show the world what we really are—few surprises.	We have important hidden sides—we can surprise people.

III Sensing and Intuition
Sensing Types or Intuitive Types

All of us are data gatherers. We need information to make our way in the world. As Jung studied human behavior, he saw two ways of perceiving things, each of which provides us with different kinds of information. We use our five senses to gather data. Our five senses collect information about things we can see, hear, feel, smell and touch. Sensing, then, deals with whatever is specific and concrete. Sensing focuses on the details, on the facts.

Intuition, on the other hand, goes beyond what is real or concrete. Intuition is what we use when we focus on meaning, possibilities and relationships. Intuition wants to know what the facts mean. Intuition seeks patterns or relationships in sensing details. Intuition wants to identify possibilities in the specifics. If sensing collects information, intuition generates it. Intuition generalizes. It identifies context and creates abstractions.

We use sensing when we:

- look for typographical errors
- notice a change in the dial tone
- smell burning leaves in the fall
- feel the temperature of the water in the shower
- taste the salt in the casserole

We use intuition when we:

- look for meaning in what someone says or does
- identify the possible benefits or risks of a course of action
- generate a new way to handle a problem
- guess the solution to a mystery
- identify a pattern in someone's behavior

Sometimes an intuitive insight sounds like a judgment. There's a simple way to distinguish between the two. Judgments either give direction to behavior, draw conclusions or ascribe a value to something. Intuition simply generates something that wasn't there. Try the following example:

A manager has an important end-of-the-day meeting with a subordinate. Soon the manager notices that her subordinate is constantly looking at his watch. After a while, the manager says to herself: "He doesn't want to be here!"

What does she do? She looks at her subordinate and says: "I notice you keep looking at your watch. Do you need to be somewhere else?"

"Oh, no. I'm sorry," responds the subordinate. "Yesterday was my birthday, and my family gave me this new watch. It still feels funny on my wrist and I keep looking at it!"

Noticing her subordinate's behavior involved sensing. Her interpretation of that behavior was an intuitive action. Note that we don't know what her judgment was. Did she judge the behavior right or wrong? Did she like or dislike the behavior? Did what she observe make her angry? Or was she relieved because she did not want to be there, either? Do we even know from her words what she would do as a result of her observation?

(Note that she did do something. She checked out her intuitive perception before judging it. We can surmise [using intuition!] that she may have said to herself: "Before I act on my hunch, I will check it out." If she did say those words, that was a judgment!)

We all go back and forth between sensing and intuition all the time. We do not use them equally or equally well. Sensing types are people who prefer sensing to intuition as their favorite way of gathering information. The gravitational pull is to the world of the specific. Sensing types are at home with details. They collect them easily and well. Their natural impulse when anything comes up is to focus on the realities.

Intuition does not come naturally to them. They prefer to use intuition only after they have built a solid base of details. When they have the details, their intuitive perceptions can be penetratingly accurate. When forced into intuition prematurely—to them—their insights can have a negative cast. Being intuitive is draining to them. They want to test intuition against the facts and often do not trust the intuitive perceptions of others.

Intuitive types live in a very different perceptual world. The natural pull for them is to move beyond the specifics to the world of context, generalization and abstraction. They want to identify the meaning in things. They are drawn to what is possible. They are more likely to be interested in sensing details when they support an exciting intuitive insight. Forced to deal directly with the facts is difficult and draining.

Some sensing types have well developed intuitive sides. They move relatively easily between both worlds, though the natural home base remains sensing. Other sensing types avoid intuition whenever they can. And the same is true for intuitives. Some are fully aware of the importance of details and develop strong sensing skills. Sensing, however, remains their acquired ability. Their natural skills are intuitive.

The best available statistics we have suggest that approximately 70% of the population are sensing types and 30% intuitive types.

The dialogues and the chart on the following pages restate and pursue further the differing worlds of sensing and intuitive types.

Sensing: I'm good at seeing "what is." What could be more important than that?

Intuition: I like looking at "what could be"—what's the use of "what is" without "what could be!"

Sensing: I'm quick to grasp the details of a situation.

Intuition: I'm quick to see the big picture.

Sensing: I must admit that sometimes I have trouble seeing the big picture.

Intuition: I'll own up to the fact that I am often tripped up by details that I haven't noticed.

Sensing: I'm realistic and practical. I've got my feet on the ground.

Intuition: I'm imaginative. I like the view from the clouds.

Sensing: No way. I prefer reality to fantasy any day.

Intuition: I'm just the other way around—I prefer fantasy to reality.

Sensing: I tend to be specific and literal when I speak, write or listen.

Intuition: I tend to be general and abstract when I speak, write or listen.

Sensing: I like to describe the facts first, and then I may—or may not!—state the general point.

Intuition: I make the general point, and then I may—or may not!—bother to describe the facts.

Sensing: I am good at seeing solutions to practical, concrete problems.

Intuition: That's not my thing. I admit I'm likely to be impatient with or ignore those kinds of problems.

Sensing: On the other hand, I'll confess, I sometimes have trouble coming up with solutions to complicated, theoretical or abstract problems —I have no patience with them, if the truth be told.

Intuition: Not me. I love to deal with those kinds of problems—the more imaginative, the better.

Sensing: I don't even like complicated theory—it makes my head swim.

Intuition: That's my world. I'm at home with theory and abstraction.

Sensing: I like to identify and work with the specifics necessary to successfully carry out an assignment.

Intuition: I wish I could do that. Most of the time I don't even want to think about those things.

Sensing: When I try to do what you are good at, I often draw blanks, feel awkward or focus on "doom and gloom" stuff.

Intuition: Well, when I try to do what you are good at, I get frustrated and impatient, miss a lot of obvious things you see, or I run off endlessly about specifics, not knowing what's important and what isn't.

Common Characteristics of Sensing Types

We see "what is."

We are quick to grasp details

We are realistic.

We prefer reality to fantasy.

We are specific and literal when speaking, writing, or listening.

We describe the facts first, and then we may (or may not!) state the general point.

We may have trouble seeing "the big picture."

We can be quick to see solutions to practical, concrete problems.

We may have trouble seeing solutions to complicated, theoretical or abstract problems.

We focus easily on the specifics necessary to successfully carry out an assignment.

We often do not like complicated theory.

Common Characteristics of Intuitive Types

We see "what could be."

We are likely to be tripped up by the details.

We are imaginative.

We prefer fantasy to reality.

We are general and abstract when speaking, writing, or listening.

We make the general point, and then we may (or may not!) describe the facts.

We are quick to see "the big picture."

We are likely to be impatient with or ignore practical, concrete problems.

We can come up with imaginative solutions to complicated, theoretical, or abstract problems.

We often do not even want to think about the specifics necessary to carry out an assignment.

We enjoy or are at home with theory and abstractions.

IV Thinking and Feeling
Thinking Types or Feeling Types

Thinking and feeling are two sharply contrasting ways of making decisions, forming judgments or arriving at conclusions. They are processes by which we judge, decide and conclude things. Of the four sets of opposites, this one often proves the most difficult to grasp. Part of the problem lies in Jung's choice of words. Thinking to most of us suggests reasoning; feeling suggests emotions.

Jung meant something quite different. He recognized human beings have the capacity to make decisions based on reason. He believed that he could identify two quite dissimilar reasoning processes. One—thinking—is based on logic. Thinking makes every attempt to look at things objectively and impersonally. It tries to keep personal bias or values out of the process. It is a process that leads to a conclusion to which the sentence can be added: "That's what logic says. It doesn't matter whether I like it or not."

The other way of making judgments—feeling—is based on a process of valuing. Feeling looks at things subjectively and personally. It is a person-centered, value-based way of forming conclusions. It is a process that, as Jung said, "arranges things in accordance with their value." It is a process that leads to a conclusion about which these words can be added: "It matters, and that's all I need to know."

This is an example of the thinking process:

A man sets out to buy a shirt. He walks right past the sport shirts, because he has more of them than he does dress shirts. He looks at the dress shirts, and picks out two white shirts because he has only one of them. Did he buy what he wanted? Who knows? We cannot tell from the reasoning process he went through.

This is an example of the feeling process:

A man sets out to buy a shirt. He looks at both the sport shirts and the dress shirts and begins to identify those that he finds attractive. He pulls them out, lays them on the counter and begins to compare each with the other until he is clear which two he likes best. He buys them. Did he buy the shirts he needed? We don't know. We cannot tell from his reasoning process.

It is important to keep in mind that thinking and feeling are processes, not end results. A decision—I am going to buy two shirts today—does not tell us anything about the process that went into it. We frequently share only our decisions, not the reasoning process behind them. For that reason, it is sometimes difficult to tell whether the process is a thinking or a feeling one. Take as an example deciding which movie to go to: Thinking looks at the newspaper to identify which the critics say is the best movie and goes to that one. Feeling studies what the critics say to identify which has more appeal.

The way we use language often gives an indication of which process we are using. Thinking uses words that make things sound impersonal:

"I don't believe anyone should . . ."

"One in that position must always keep in mind . . ."

"A father has a responsibility . . ."

"Effective managers do not . . ."

Feeling judgments, on the other hand, make frequent use of words like:

"care about"

"matters to me"

"like" or "dislike"

"appreciate" or "don't appreciate"

"want" or "don't want"

We use a thinking process when we:

- compare a set of financial statements against standards established by the auditing profession to determine if the standards were met.

- check a consumer research magazine to identify which is the best product and buy it.

- establish criteria for grading papers, apply the criteria, and give grades.

- establish what work needs to be finished to justify a vacation and then taking it only if the work is done.

- decide whether to buy a camera by weighing the costs against how much use it will get.

The common thread in each of the above examples is that once the standards or criteria are set, the process of weighing things against those standards leaves out any personal values.

We use a feeling process when we:

- decide that our friends are more important than the reputation of a college and use that criteria to decide which college to go to.

- stay within the 55 mile-per-hour limit because we care more about not getting a ticket than we care about how fast we will get where we are going.

- decide not to tell someone that we don't like what they are doing because what matters more to us is to avoid upsetting them.

- identify which is more important to us in an important election—the candidate or the party.

- decide not to buy a car because we did not like what we see as a clash between the color of the car's exterior and interior.

The common thread in all the feeling examples is the direct weighing of values. The key question in all of them is which value should guide the decision making process?

Simple decisions, like the examples of buying shirts, can be "pure." That is, they can be strictly thinking or feeling. Most complex decisions, on the other hand, use both. When logic sets the parameters, when logic governs the overall process, then the decision is a thinking one. When a valuing process governs, then the decision is a feeling one.

We all use both ways of making decisions, but we do not use them equally or equally well. We trust one process more than the other. We can go through a complex reasoning process that uses both. If we prefer thinking to feeling, the feeling judgments will be small pieces of an overall thinking process. If we prefer feeling to thinking, the thinking judgments will be brief forays into logic. The context is feeling.

We can have a "pure" thinking judgment about something and a "pure" feeling judgment about the same thing. If the two arrive at the same conclusion, we are most sure of ourselves, we are most comfortable with the decision. If the two go in opposite directions, we may pause a moment. But if we prefer thinking to feeling, we will not listen to a feeling decision that contradicts a strongly held thinking decision. And, of course, it is just the opposite for those who prefer feeling to thinking.

In the first of the two examples that follow, the writer is a feeling type. He based his decision to buy a new car by weighing which he liked less—driving an old, beat-up automobile in poor mechanical condition or making the payments on a new car. His decision to buy the car he bought was based on what he liked. There are "little" thinking decisions that entered into the process, most clearly his checking with *Consumer Reports* in the last stage of his decision-making process.

Feeling

Three years ago, I was driving a six-year-old Toyota Corolla. It started to have mechanical problems. When I drove up hills, it would lose power, even to the point that in first gear it would barely make it up the hill.

I took it to a garage and spent approximately $50 for a repair. It worked OK for a while but then the problem returned. I took it back for a $150 repair. Again it worked for a while but then started acting up again.

I have always liked new things and fantasize a lot about getting and having a "new" car.

I suddenly noticed that when my anger and frustration with my car problems was high and the more it continued, my reality about buying a new car was more concrete.

At some point in this process, I can review what has gone on and say that I had decided to buy a new car.

But although in my heart the decision was made, I began a process to validate and justify the decision. I took it in for one more repair that did not work.

I shared my frustration with friends and told them I was thinking of getting a new car. I asked their advice. Of course, I mostly asked friends who I knew would support my desire.

I checked and rechecked my finances to verify if I had enough money for a new car payment.

I noticed other things about my car that I didn't like— unrepaired dents, worn tires, etc.

I reached a point where I had gathered a critical mass of "facts" to support my emotional feelings. It became obvious—it not only "felt" right—the facts *demanded* that I get a new car.

In my fantasy life I had decided 3 years before what type of car I wanted to buy based on repair record—I don't like being frustrated and angry over an unreliable and expensive car—and what "looked" good to me.

I wanted a Honda Accord. I then checked *Consumer Reports* to verify the repair record, went to a dealership with an idea of how much I wanted to spend, and ordered the car I wanted.

In the second example, the writer is a thinking type. She clearly steps over into feeling to establish some of the criteria she used in deciding which apartment to rent. The overall approach, however, is impersonal, logical and analytical.

Thinking

I was moving out of a house in San Rafael and planning to move into an apartment. I decided to make a list of items that I wanted:

1. No commute—wide surface streets between apartment and work.

2. Rent range.

3. I identified four neighborhoods I liked. I wanted a quiet neighborhood, varied, central.

4. I identified specific needs in an apartment (size, closets, utilities, type of kitchen [gas appliances], utility room or utility hook-up, style, fireplace, ocean view).

5. I wanted a garage so no parking hassles.

6. I listed the questions I needed to ask (e.g. heating bills, etc.)

Once my list was made, I took a weekend to drive through the neighborhoods that I'd listed looking for apartments that were for rent. On Sunday, I checked the classified ads and rated apartments for rent that were within the rent range and in the neighborhoods. I found three. Two were open and I called the third for an appointment. I took my list and evaluated the apartments according to my criteria. I made notes on each one including the "feel of the place." Once back home, I reviewed the notes, tallied up the check marks. One place had all but two of the criteria. I called the owner back and negotiated for one of the items and decided I could live without the last one. I also had to get specific facts that I'd not remembered, though I'd checked them off. The following weekday, I rented the apartment.

People who prefer thinking to feeling work hard to look at things objectively and impersonally. As a result, they become very good at following the content of any situation or discussion. On the other hand, they do not have equal skills at seeing the feeling, or personal issues. They are often unaware of their own or others' personal reactions. As a result they can be unaware of how their words or behavior are affecting others. They can be unaware of the emotional state in back of the words or behavior of others.

People who prefer feeling to thinking do the opposite. They work hard to see things in personal and subjective terms. Thus, they are sensitive to their own and others' feelings. They may, in fact, miss some of the impersonal content of a situation or discussion because they have focused so strongly on the people considerations.

The best available statistics we have suggest that the general population is equally divided between thinking and feeling types. This is the only set of preferences for which there seems to be a difference in the distribution according to sex. Approximately 60% of the male population is thinking, and 60% of the female population is feeling. Our culture's sex role stereotyping encourages males to be thinking and females to be feeling.

The dialogues and chart on the following pages review how the thinking and feeling preference affects our behavior.

Thinking: Whenever I make a decision, I look for principles to guide me. The kind of principles I seek are basic truths, laws, or assumptions that are generally accepted or proven. When I make a decision, I want to know what's "right" in a situation like this.

Feeling: I look at a decision quite differently. I look at the specific situation or decision and then sort out the values that are involved—my own personal values and the values of the people or institutions that matter to me. Then I apply those values and see where they lead me.

Thinking: When I make a decision, I use my principles—and being logical is one of my most important principles—to link things together. That's why my decisions have an "if . . ., then" quality to them.

Feeling: My decisions link things together according to their value—either to me or to others or to the institutions of which I am a part. That's why my decisions have an "I value . . ., it matters" quality to them.

Thinking: When I make a decision, I focus on the content, on the "what" that is involved. I do my best to depersonalize everything.

Feeling: I think it's important to take personal considerations into account when making decisions.

Thinking: I try to screen out of my decisions my own emotions and the emotions of others. Decisions based on emotions seem wrong to me.

Feeling: I find it difficult to focus exclusively on the content of a decision, as you call it. People's emotions are part of the content of a good decision.

Thinking: Not to me. I am uncomfortable with decisions that involve my own emotions and those of others—I will even avoid discussing these kinds of things.

Feeling: And I'm uncomfortable with decisions that require ignoring my own emotions and those of others. I am good at bringing these issues into a decision-making process in useful ways.

Thinking: I am analytically oriented in my decisions. I like analyzing things impersonally. I listen carefully to people's thoughts and am quick to see either the usefulness of an idea or its weakness, and I like being able to share my judgments on what other people say. I am told that I often do not pay sufficient attention to people when I make decisions, but if logic tells me this or that is the way to go, shouldn't people just see and accept that?

Feeling: Not always. People are important, too. I believe in being people-oriented when I make decisions. I like listening to what other people care about. I reflect on how their values fit with my own. And I like it when my decisions can support and bring out the best in people. Sometimes I'm told that it's necessary to leave people considerations out of my decision making, but that's difficult for me to do.

Thinking: I am often told that my decisions and the way I express them hurt people—often I am not even aware of that until someone points it out to me.

Feeling: It's natural to me to have my decisions and the way I express them reflect a sensitivity to people.

Thinking: When decisions call for it, I can reprimand or fire people.

Feeling: That is not one of my strengths. I even have difficulty telling people anything unpleasant.

Thinking: In decisions that affect me, I need to know that I have been treated fairly. I can accept a lot so long as I know that.

Feeling: In decisions that affect me, I need to know that I am appreciated. I need and want praise. When I know that I am appreciated, I do my best work. As a student, I do my best for teachers who like me.

Thinking: I am not always aware that my decisions can create conflict. Sometimes when I am aware, I don't care very much. I can get along without a lot of harmony.

Feeling: I am always concerned when decisions involve conflict. I like harmony, and I know how to surface and resolve conflict. I am often negatively affected in conflict situations.

Thinking: I am good at exploring the logical, impersonal consequences of actions or decisions.

Feeling: I am good at assessing the human impact of actions or decisions.

Thinking: When I try to do what you are good at, I have an uneasy feeling that I am making a biased decision, and that seems all wrong to me—it won't stand up in court! So when I sense those kinds of decisions popping up in my head, I generally try to ignore them.

Feeling: And when I try to do what you are good at, I feel as if somehow I am leaving out the things that really matter. Sometimes those decisions remind me of the auto safety commercials: "He had the right of way. He was right. Dead right." So I tend to ignore those kinds of decisions even when I'm aware that I have them.

Common Characteristics of Thinking Types

In our decision making, we seek to identify and apply principles of right and and wrong—principles that have universal applicability.

Our decisions link things by logical, impersonal constructs.

We focus on the content involved in a decision.

We screen out of our decision making our own emotions and the emotions of others.

We are uncomfortable with decisions that involve our own emotions and the emotions of others; we avoid discussing these issues.

We are analytically oriented in our decisions—we respond more easily to people's thoughts.

Our decisions and the way we express them may hurt people without our being aware of it.

When decisions call for it, we can reprimand people or fire them.

In decisions that affect us, we need to know that we have been treated fairly.

We are not often upset when decisions involve conflict; we can get along without harmony.

We are good at exploring the logical, impersonal consequences of actions or decisions.

Common Characteristics of Feeling Types

In our decision making, we sort out and and apply our own personal values and the values of people or institutions that matter to us.

Our decisions link things according to their value.

We think of personal considerations when we make decisions.

We find it difficult to focus exclusively on the content of a decision.

We are uncomfortable with decisions that require ignoring our own emotions and the emotions of others; we know how to bring these issues into the decision-making process.

We are more people oriented in our decisions—we respond more easily to people's values.

Our decisions and the way we express them reflect a sensitivity to their impact on people.

When decisions call for it, we have difficulty telling people unpleasant things.

In decisions that affect us, we need to be appreciated—to be praised.

We are sensitive to situations involving conflict, often know how to surface and and resolve conflict, and can be negatively affected when conflict is ignored.

We are good at assessing the human impact of actions or decisions.

V Judging and Perceiving
Judging Types or Perceiving Types

Briggs and Myers believed that Jung implied a fourth set of opposites, so they added it to their interpretation of Jung's type theory. Judging and perceiving deal with how we relate to the world around us. They describe an attitude toward the external world and define how we orient ourselves to that world.

Judging wants the external world organized and orderly. Judging looks at that world and sees decisions that need to be made. Judging makes plans about how to manage the extraverted environment. Having established a plan, judging wants things to move along in accordance with that plan. Judging wants things settled. In short, judging wants to form and express judgments about the world.

Perceiving is quite different. Perceiving wants to understand the world, not judge it. It wants to be free to move with whatever comes up. Perceiving wants to collect information and to explore options. Perceiving wants to interact with the extraverted environment in a flexible, spontaneous and adaptable way.

We operate out of a judging attitude when we:

- make a plan for the day
- decide what we will eat during the week, make up a shopping list and go to the grocery store
- organize others to get a job done
- move a conversation to closure so that we can go on to another topic and settle that one
- express a judgment

We operate out of a perceiving attitude when we:

- explore alternatives
- ask others for information
- postpone a decision to find out what other options are available
- react spontaneously to new information
- act comfortably without a plan or schedule

We all feel both of these gravitational pulls. There are times when we want our extraverted environments to be organized, when we want things to be settled, when we feel the need to make and follow plans. There are also times when we want to go with the flow of things, when we want to wait to decide until we have more information, when we want to explore options. There are times when we want to judge things, and there are times when we want to understand things.

We do not, however, feel the gravitational pull equally. We are drawn to one of these opposites. If we are drawn more to the judging polarity, our natural impulse is to want things in the extraverted world to be settled. We make and express judgments about what goes on in that world. A good day for us is when we have made a plan and at the end of the day we have accomplished those things that we have set out to do. We are unsettled, dislocated—we feel out of control—if things keep disrupting our plans. Control of the external environment is a constant concern. We are not as comfortable sharing information as we are judgments. Our perceiving nature—our desire for spontaneity— emerges most often when we have done so much planning and struggling to keep up with plans that we are tired and want a rest.

If we are drawn more to the perceiving polarity, our natural impulse is to want to postpone decisions, to explore options. We like to find out about things—it's often fun to learn something new. We don't usually have a strong need to do something with the information we collect. We've had a good day when we have been busy all day and have reacted effectively to whatever has come up. We become tentative when sharing judgments—we have to be ready to change them given new

Judging: I work best when I can plan my work and follow my plan. I know when things need to be organized and settled. I know how to make lists, and I like making them and crossing things off.

Perceiving: I'm not into that. I want to be able to adapt to what comes up. I get my energy from new situations, and I am good at responding to them.

Judging: That doesn't fit me. I feel dislocated when things come up unexpectedly. I don't like it when I am confronted with a problem or opportunity that means I may have to choose between following my plan or doing something else. Sometimes, I'll admit, I wish I felt free to do just whatever comes up. More often than not, though, I find myself wishing the unexpected would go away!

Perceiving: And I'm just the opposite. I feel hemmed in if I have to make or follow a schedule. When I do make a list, which isn't very often, it can sit around forever because I put such vague or ambitious things on it—and I almost never follow it because I am so busy doing other things. And you know what? When I do make lists, I very often promptly lose them!

Now, it is true that when I get really overcommitted or when I have too many options I sometimes wish I could exercise more control, get more discipline in my life, and make your lists and stick to them! But I'll bet I'd soon get bored and wish something exciting would come up that I could respond to!

Judging: Can't we settle things?

Perceiving: Can't we keep our options open a little longer?

Common Characteristics of Judging Types	**Common Characteristics of Perceiving Types**
We work best when we can plan our work and follow our plan.	We adapt well to changing situations—are energized by situations and can respond resourcefully.
We like to get things settled and finished.	We do not mind leaving things open for alterations.
We may decide things too quickly.	We may have trouble making decisions.
We may cling too long to a plan or a list.	We may not make or follow lists or plans even when the situation calls for them.
We may dislike interrupting the project we are on for a more urgent one.	We may start too many projects and have difficulty finishing them.
We may not notice new things that need to be done.	We may postpone unpleasant tasks.
We want to get right to the point	We want all available data.
We tend to be satisfied once we have reached a judgment on a thing, situation or person.	We tend to be curious and welcome new light on a thing, situation or person.
We are time and deadline oriented.	We tend to think there is plenty of time.
We feel time pressures early.	We feel time pressures late.

VI People and the Preferences

How do people who share preferences get along? And what about those whose preferences differ? To give comprehensive answers to these questions would take another book—or books. Human behavior is, in the final analysis, much too complex for any theory, however rich, to give more than suggestive answers. Nonetheless, Jung's theory gives us many useful insights.

It is important to keep in mind that people who share preferences can get along famously, or they can be at genuine loggerheads with each other. They can also become boring to one another. The same is true for those whose preferences differ. With these caveats, let's examine briefly each of the four sets of preferences:

Extraversion/Introversion: When extraverts and introverts collide, extraverts complain that introverts won't ever let them know what they are thinking. Introverts see extraverts as intrusive and unnecessarily talkative. When the relationship is a good one, extraverts appreciate the reflective nature of introverts, and introverts like the way extraverts draw them out.

When extraverts get along, they energize each other. When introverts get along, they give each other the time to tune in to inner thoughts. As one introvert said to the other after they had been driving in silence for some miles: "This is what two introverts sound like when they're having a rich conversation!"

When extraverts clash, it's often because they are competing with each other and wearing each other out. When an introverted relationship falls apart, it is sometimes because those involved become stubbornly convinced of the validity of their inner thought processes. Neither will budge. Or they can need to talk through issues but be unwilling to do so. Or each can demand that the other do extraverted things neither wants to do.

Sensing/Intuition: This set of preferences produces some powerful misunderstandings. Sensing types often dismiss intuitives as dealing in a world of senseless unreality or meaningless abstraction. Intuitives can become very impatient with the sensing focus on and need for details.

They each may feel inadequate when with the other. Intuitives don't focus on the details and don't remember them. A sensing type doesn't understand this and can say with undisguised scorn: "I just told you . . ." and restate some details that went right past the intuitive. On the other hand, intuitives often don't go step-by-step. As one intuitive put it, "we jump lily pads." Intuitives can get very impatient with sensing types who don't operate at the same level. "I just won't repeat myself for her," said one arrogant intuitive of a sensing friend. "I know she understands what I mean. When she keeps asking me to repeat myself, she just doesn't want to accept what I say."

When sensing and intuitive types get along, it is usually because each respects the strengths of the other. An intuitive for whom it is important to communicate, can appreciate a sensing type who points out where the intuitive has become unclear. A sensing type can appreciate the ability of an intuitive who can listen to and suggest useful possibilities.

When sensing types enjoy each other, it is often because they can each build upon the other's realities. They each trust the facts, and they respect the other's competence with them. Intuitives often enjoy each other in much the same way. They each respect the other's insights and energize and spark each other to discover even richer ones.

Sensing types can bore each other, and so can intuitives. When sensing types collide, it's often because they just know the other's facts are inaccurate or incomplete. With intuitives, each can treat the other's insights with scorn.

Thinking/Feeling: When these two preferences clash, feeling often accuses thinking of being cold, unfeeling, harshly judgmental, uncaring, and out of touch with their own and others' emotions. Thinking sees feeling as illogical, emotion-driven, unwilling to engage in debate, and always trying to shift the focus of the discussion.

When the two have an effective and harmonious relationship, it is, as with other preferences, because each appreciates the other's point of view. Thinking appreciates the quickness with which feeling sees the people implications of a thinker's decisions. Feeling recognizes the thinker's ability to focus on the content and analyze it impersonally. They each bring problems to the other to get a usefully different perspective.

When thinkers work well together, they appreciate the clarity of each other's thinking. They can often anticipate each other or build on each other's logic. When feeling types enjoy each other it's often because they find that they value the same things. Each can bring a different value perspective.

When thinkers collide, it's often because they fail to recognize that each may be starting from different premises. They believe their logic is correct, the other's is wrong. Feeling types can part company over feeling betrayed, or they can run into a very powerful clash of personal values.

Judging/Perceiving: The desire for closure is as strong in judging types as is the desire for options in perceiving types. Therein lies the potential clash between these two. When judging types push for closure, perceiving types feel trapped. When perceiving types won't plan or when they change plans, judging types feel disoriented. When they clash, and they often do, it's very difficult to deal with. Neither will back off. Neither will attempt to see the world through the other's eyes. Neither will accept the other's needs as legitimate. There is no meeting half-way.

When the two relate well together, it's probably because each has a degree of flexibility. Judging types who are not rigidly wedded to their plans and schedules enjoy the spontaneous excitement perceiving types can bring. Perceiving types who appreciate the need for plans and schedules value their judging friends or associates who contribute structure to their lives.

Judging types often find other judging types comfortable to be with. They each respect the other's need for having things settled. They help each other meet those needs. Perceiving types who enjoy each other feed off each other's spontaneity. They do not try to trap the other. They accept the other's need for keeping options open. They both enjoy spur-of-the-moment activities and decisions.

When judging types do not get along, there is often a clash between equally rigidly held judgments. When judging types disagree, they often simply repeat their judgments—louder. They can also fall apart because their plans or schedules clash and neither is willing to budge.

With perceiving types, a falling out can occur because both are so unplanned and unscheduled that they each keep missing the other. Neither will accept responsibility for making a commitment. They keep dancing past each other. One begins to see the other as hopelessly undependable, not worth having a relationship with.

This brief review only touches the surface of the many ways people with the same or different preferences enjoy or struggle with each other. Jung, Briggs and Myers have put a powerful tool in our hands if we choose to use it. We can use what they have created to understand ourselves and others better, to build bridges, not walls, between us.

Chapter 2 When Preferences Combine: The Descriptions

I Introduction

Each of the sets of preferences, as we have seen, can be looked at separately. Each provides insights into our behavior. There are sixteen possible combinations of the four sets of preferences. They are:

ISTJ	**ISFJ**	**INFJ**	**INTJ**
introvert	introvert	introvert	introvert
sensing	sensing	intuition	intuition
thinking	feeling	feeling	thinking
judging	judging	judging	judging

ISTP	**ISFP**	**INFP**	**INTP**
introvert	introvert	introvert	introvert
sensing	sensing	intuition	intuition
thinking	feeling	feeling	thinking
perceiving	perceiving	perceiving	perceiving

ESTP	**ESFP**	**ENFP**	**ENTP**
extravert	extravert	extravert	extravert
sensing	sensing	intuition	intuition
thinking	feeling	feeling	thinking
perceiving	perceiving	perceiving	perceiving

ESTJ	**ESFJ**	**ENFJ**	**ENTJ**
extravert	extravert	extravert	extravert
sensing	sensing	intuition	intuition
thinking	feeling	feeling	thinking
judging	judging	judging	judging

Keirsey's four temperament groupings combine two of the four sets of preferences. They are:

SJ Traditionalist/Stabilizers	SP Troubleshooter/Negotiators
ESTJ	ESTP
ISTJ	ISTP
ESFJ	ESFP
ISFJ	ISFP

NT Visionaries	NF Catalysts
ENTJ	ENFJ
INTJ	INFJ
ENTP	ENFP
INTP	INFP

Many people are puzzled about the lack of a logical pattern in Keirsey's temperament combinations. With two of the temperaments (SJ and SP), the second preference combines with the fourth, while with the other two (NT and NF), the second preference combines with the third. But Keirsey wasn't looking for logical patterns when he studied the possible connections between temperament theory and type. He was attempting to find out whether there was any relationship between temperament and the types, and that's how the relationship fell out.

The descriptions in the pages that follow are grouped around Keirsey's temperaments.

1.   SJ: ESTJ,   ISTJ,   ESFJ,   ISFJ.

2.   SP: ESTP,   ISTP,   ESFP,   ISFP.

3.   NT: ENTJ,   INTJ,   ENTP,   INTP.

4.   NF: ENFJ,   INFJ,   ENFP,   INFP.

II The SJ Temperament

Four of the sixteen types share preferences for sensing and judging (ESTJ, ESFJ, ISTJ, and ISFJ). These types constitute one of Keirsey's four temperament styles. They view the world from the perspective of specific details and practical realities. They share a desire to make decisions about what they see. They want to organize the world they feel responsible for. Their focus on details goes beyond the here-and-now. They store and remember details about the past, and they are concerned about the future. They want to be sure that they have a correct grasp of the facts.

To SJs, realities are just that—realities. SJs accept them as such. They do not fight or ignore them. They organize them, and they take pleasure in their handiwork. Thus, they go about what they do best—organizing the details of life.

SJs often derive their sense of self in terms of the institutions or groups to which they belong. In short, they have a powerful drive to contribute to those organizations they find meaningful and important. It is for this reason that Keirsey calls the SJ temperament Traditionalists and Stabilizers.

SJs are unusually aware of the customs and traditions of the groups to which they belong. They work hard to maintain and live by them. Through their organizing skills, they bring stability to the organizations and groups of which they are a part. SJs are conservers and preservers. More consistently than other temperaments, SJs volunteer their time for community, social, or church groups. From scouts to scout leaders is a common path for many SJs. The phrase "pillars of" the church or community describes the day-to-day, steady, and enduring contributions that many SJs make to important organizations in their communities.

SJs' sensitivity to customs and traditions makes them particularly sensitive to what might be called "the acceptable thing to do." They know—or want to know—what is appropriate or within the rules, traditions, habits and customs of their organization or group. They live as much as possible within those constraints and believe that others should do so as well.

They believe that there should be rules and guidelines to govern behavior. They participate in formulating, monitoring and, if necessary, enforcing them. SJs respect authority. They expect that when they are in positions of authority others will give them the same respect.

SJs are solid, grounded, practical and dependable. When they make plans or commitments, they follow through if at all possible. They have a realistic picture of time and task. They know what they can do within a given period of time. An SJ wife, for example, watched her husband type his doctoral dissertation under tight time pressure. From the beginning, she urged him to divide the number of pages he was typing per hour by the pages in the dissertation. He needed, she believed, to establish—and keep to—a work schedule. Until almost too late, he refused to do so. When he did, he found he had fallen so far behind that he had to type for 72 hours straight to finish. His SJ wife knew, long before he did, that he wasn't working fast enough.

SJs make detailed plans—for work or play—well in advance. Once made, they may not be happy at having them disrupted. There is a poster that contains the words "Life is what happens to you when you're making other plans." It is not one that SJs would want to buy and hang on their walls!

Many SJs make effective use of lists to help them order the details of a day or a task. Their lists do not contain vague statements. They do not contain descriptions of tasks so complex or complicated that they cannot address and cross them off. Rather, they break tasks down into manageable units. They want to track their progress and feel a sense of accomplishment as they cross off one item after another.

In approaching any task, SJs want to know the details. They want to be as specific as possible when providing information. In fact, SJs can be embarrassed when they cannot be as precise as they believe they should be.

"How many people are going to be at the workshop you want me to conduct," said an NT management trainer to an SJ colleague. For his planning purposes, he needed only an estimate.

"Oh, gee, I'm not sure," responded the SJ, clearly upset at herself. "Is it . . . 23 or 24. I just don't remember. I'm sorry. I'll find out and let you know as soon as I get back to the office."

It is easy to draw the conclusion that SJs are cautious, conservative, conforming, risk-avoiding people. Many SJs are just that. But the judgment is incomplete. There are SJ males, for example, who want to be part of what might be called a "macho" culture. Some join groups that get involved in risk-taking adventures. Others join groups where the "rule" is to rebel against authority. Still others may make male-only drinking-buddy groups an important part of their lives.

There are many SJs who have a sense of freedom and adventure. Though they might not by themselves think of doing something unusual or impetuous, they may enthusiastically join others who do. And many SJs have an occasional impulse to do something new and exciting.

Many SJs like the motto "If it ain't broke, don't fix it." That does not mean, however, that SJs are consistently resistant to change. Though not by nature initiators of change, they can be powerful reformers. First, they need to be convinced—and some SJs take a lot of convincing!—that their organizations are not operating effectively. And SJs don't always get credit for the many unpaid overtime hours they work to achieve the important incremental improvements that keep an organization running smoothly.

SJs can be successful and even daring entrepreneurs. They keep their eyes on business opportunities. They master the relevant information. They pay close attention to timing. And when the opportunity is there, they move quickly and surely. And they follow through.

SJs often undervalue themselves. Their sense of responsibility is such that they take for granted much of what they do. They can be very self critical—unforgiving, even—when they believe that they have not lived up to their responsibilities. They go about their work in such an unassuming way that others take them for granted, too.

SJs often view others the same way they view themselves. They pay little attention to the good work that others do. Good work, after all, is just a part of the job. What's important is to point out when others are not fulfilling their responsibilities or commitments. There is an exception—SJs are least likely of all temperaments to forget those formal occasions when awards, rewards, and congratulations are given out. That is another responsibility—another tradition—that SJs can be counted on to fulfill.

SJs and the World of Work

It is not at all uncommon for SJs—particularly STJs—to become managers. They have many natural managerial skills. They attend to the details. They want closure. They are good at making plans and schedules. They consistently follow through. They are dependable. They bring order and stability to their work units. They pay attention to the day-to-day work procedures. They clarify, revise or enforce policies, rules and regulations when necessary to maintain a smooth-running organization.

Just as SJs are meticulous about knowing and following the rules, they expect others to feel the same way. In what must surely be an extreme example, but one that makes the point, an SJ manager made a mid-morning appointment with an internal consultant. When the two got together, the SJ asked the consultant if he wanted a cup of coffee. When the consultant could not be persuaded to take any, the SJ manager looked a little uncomfortable and said: "What I want to talk with you about is not work related. It's difficult for me to justify doing that on work hours. But the rules say we are entitled to a 15 minute break in the morning. So as long as it's coffee-break time and we're drinking coffee, I feel a little better about it!" Though the SJ manager tried to make light of what he was saying, it clearly did matter to him to be strictly business-like during the entire work day.

Like other temperaments, SJs seek management positions that make use of their strengths. Positions that involve the administrative functions of an organization—finance, audit, administrative services, for example—often attract SJs. SJs provide particularly effective leadership for organizations that have recently undergone significant upheavals and need a period of regrouping and stability. Organizations that have been caught in the turmoil of unethical or illegal practices may turn to a strong SJ, who will work hard to restore the tarnished image of the corporation or organization. In the peacetime army, general officers are often SJs. The desire to be part of meaningful social institutions and to be of service to others leads some SJs into the ministry. And the country has benefitted from the solid and stabilizing leadership of men like George Washington, Dwight D. Eisenhower, and Gerald R. Ford, all of whom may have been SJs.

All temperaments, each in different ways, produce leadership qualities that under certain conditions capture people's imaginations and inspire devotion. Leaders who have these qualities are often described as having charisma. Turmoil often surrounds charismatic leaders. Sometimes they create it by virtue of their visions. Sometimes the turmoil is there because they have assumed leadership positions in times of crisis. SJs can have a unique form of charisma. Theirs is the leadership that brings calm back after the storm. Theirs is the leadership that brings relief from the charisma of others. To provide relief from charisma can be a form of charisma. It can be a special kind of leadership that captures the imagination and devotion of a weary and grateful people.

SJs are often described as liking routine. Usually it's intuitive types who are doing the describing. It's an inaccurate judgment, one that results from confusing process and content. SJs are good with detail. That's content. Intuitives pay more attention to the process—to how the content is handled. When intuitives look at a job, they see the process. SJs see the content. Thus, intuitives see repetition, SJs see variety. To intuitives, the job of a bank teller, for example, is dull. So is one that involves auditing accounts or providing human services information to citizens in need of help. To SJs, who focus on the details, no situation is exactly the same. These jobs are not dull at all to them.

It is true that SJs do not usually like positions where everything is constantly in flux. They want roots, and they want stability. Too much change is chaos to them. Too much change is both bewildering and dislocating. At work, in the home, as parents or children, SJs need what they themselves are so good at providing—consistency, reliability, predictability, stability.

An internationally experienced organizational consultant who is apparently not familiar with the work of Jung and Keirsey nevertheless finds that managers seem to fit into four quite distinct categories. The categories have a remarkable resemblance to Keirsey's temperaments. He uses the term "Administrator" for one group when they are productive and effective. Administrators are the ones who insure that systems work the way they were designed to work. They attend to the important day-to-day workings of the organization. They excel at organizing the details.

He has a harsher term—"Bureaucrat"—when the rules and regulations become more important than the mission of the organization. Bureaucrats can block an organization's productivity by developing ever more complicated procedures that must be followed at all costs. Bureaucrats remind one of the story of the person who asked his friend the librarian how things were going at work. "Oh, just great," said the librarian. "We have only two books out and one's coming back tomorrow." Administrators and Bureaucrats sound like another name for Keirsey's SJ temperament.

SJs are not usually interested in abstract theories or in long range thinking. Activities involving abstract conceptualization or planning for a future far away seem too much like idle speculation to SJs. They concentrate their time and energy on the present or the immediate, foreseeable future. Those things are concrete for SJs. They seldom have the interest, time, energy, or patience for a world of improbables.

An SJ president of a community association in a new, fast-growing planned community devotes her attention to bringing a fragmented board together. She concentrates her energy on addressing pressing issues confronting the community. She spends her time marshalling a host of volunteer experts to represent the community to local and state governments. She gives speeches and makes presentations to other community groups.

She does not involve herself in issues like the long-range implications of dwindling association membership. She does not wonder about how to attract new members to the association when the "new town" image wanes. She does not think about how present conditions may be pointing to significant and serious problems several years away.

SJ Children and Students

SJ children and students, unless they get involved in groups whose norms prescribe otherwise, know the rules and follow them. They work hard to live up to the responsibilities given them. They belong to and become important parts of clubs and other groups. They are often the delight of parents and teachers alike. They do their chores. They hand in homework assignments on time and in good form. They are attentive and respectful of authority. They make steady progress at home, in school, in life. To do well, however, SJ children need stability. They may not respond well to conflict among adults or to instability in the home. A divorce may be particularly unsettling for SJ children.

Young SJs want parents, teachers and other adults to provide specific and concrete guidance. They are unhappy with adults who avoid making decisions or who cannot be counted on to fulfill promises. Some young SJs may try to insist on having their needs met. Failing that, they may express their frustration, anger, hurt, or confusion.

Some adults may view the need of SJ young people for explicit guidance as a sign of dependence. They may see the SJ need for having even "little" things settled as a sign of immaturity. That is not the case. To attempt to change these behaviors, or to criticize them, is a mistake. SJs consciously or unconsciously will experience that as a denial of their essential selves. Like other temperaments, SJs need a supportive environment, one that enables them to fulfill the promise of their temperament.

SJ Adults and Parents

As mates, SJs run a well-organized home. They take family celebrations, anniversaries, and birthdays seriously. They make early plans for vacations and entertainment. They make sure that the family lives within its budget. They put money aside for a rainy day. They want to know where their children are at anytime of the day or night. They will be either very anxious or very upset with them for not leaving word about where they can be found.

Treats, vacations, frivolity, nights out are earned and planned. They participate in—perhaps organize—the neighborhood picnic on Memorial or Labor Day . They do the traditional things at Christmas or on New Year's Eve. They may enjoy a certain amount of spontaneity or unpredictable behavior from their mates, but not so much that it threatens the stability of hearth and home.

As parents, SJs lay down the rules and expect children to follow them. For children of different temperaments, SJ parents may set too many rules. They may be too confining, too quick to punish unacceptable behavior. When children do not do what is expected, SJ parents are likely to become upset. They see their children's behavior as somehow a reflection on them as parents. They wonder where they went wrong. They take their parenting role seriously. Some SJ mothers may define themselves in terms of that role and be particularly at a loss when their children leave the nest.

A Final Word

Life is a serious journey for SJs Hard-working, dependable, keepers-of-the-traditions, stabilizers of home, community and work, SJs, often quietly and unassumingly, are the glue that holds society together. Often taken for granted or criticized for slowing down "progress," SJs deserve more credit than they get—or give themselves.

ESTJ

ESTJs focus their energies on the world around them. They make quick, crisp, impersonal and practical judgments about everything and anything they see. They are take-charge people. They like being "the boss". They enjoy the power that goes with leadership. They take leadership roles seriously and work hard to exercise responsible stewardship. ESTJs, says Myers, "will run as much of the world as is theirs to run". Von Franz adds: "This type is to be found among organizers, people in high office and government positions, in business, in law and among scientists."

ESTJs like things kept practical, concrete, and impersonal. They want their worlds organized and orderly, and they are good at following through. They are frequently hard-working, "no frills, " "no-nonsense" people.

For many ESTJs, to have a judgment is to express it. Some have little sensitivity to how their judgments affect others. They can hurt other people's feelings without knowing it. Some ESTJs, when that is pointed out to them, don't really care. They are likely to view the problem as something wrong with the other person, not with what they said or how they expressed themselves. Some ESTJs are sharply and consistently critical of others. They are difficult to be around.

Many ESTJs, however, learn to moderate their judgments. These ESTJs are often fun to be with. They have a lot of charm. They are outgoing by nature, and when work is done, they enjoy a good time. They are often a source of good stories or the latest jokes. They balance their serious approach to work and life with a sense of playfulness that is engaging. They are both earnest and light-hearted. They take their responsibilities seriously, but not themselves.

ESTJs' attention to detail and their need for order make them excellent at what might be called maintenance functions. They bring to whatever they do a recognition of the importance of having things run smoothly and efficiently. They believe that work should be well done and completed on time. They are hard workers. They know how to organize themselves and others to get the job done. They take a sound, practical and conservative (that is, conserving) approach to work and life.

Many ESTJs extend their conserving ways to their important possessions. They like material things, and they work hard to keep them looking new and functioning in top condition. They are likely to dress carefully and well. They are often dapper dressers. Homes, automobiles, clothes, accessories—all these can be matters of pride to ESTJs. Their possessions are extensions of themselves, and they treat them as such. One young ESTJ accountant owns a large, American-made car. Though several years old, he keeps it neat and polished. When he parks it at work in the hot Texas sun, he carefully brings out of the trunk a huge canvas cover, which he meticulously puts over his car!

In work or occupations where success is often measured in terms of attention to detail, some ESTJs are risk-taking entrepreneurs—often very successful ones. They master all the facts. They think through where bold moves are likely to be successful. They lay thorough foundations. Then they act, fully aware that ultimate success depends on their persistent, careful follow-through.

ESTJs are not likely to have much patience with theory. They often equate it with idle speculation. In fact, many ESTJs have trouble understanding those who do not view the world the way they do. For them, things are either black or white. Grey is a color they don't easily understand. An ENFP may have been thinking of ESTJs when he wrote a friend: "It must be difficult to have a true-and-false mind in a multiple-choice world." Some ESTJs have short fuses and explosive tempers when dealing with people or things that do not conform to their view of how things should be.

Logical decisions about people and things are ESTJs' greatest strength. Sorting out what matters to them, and being sensitive to others' feelings, is the least developed side of their personalities. They often have trouble understanding their own emotions. They do not have natural skills at dealing with others' emotions. Judgments based on subjective values make them uneasy. They often do not know how to relate to those who decide things that way. Expressions of emotion can leave them embarrassed and at a loss as to how to respond.

On the other hand, most ESTJs have a sentimental streak that they keep well hidden. It finds expression in patriotism, strong feelings about family traditions, or even an emotionally powerful movie or theater performance. Underneath that sometimes prickly exterior, there often lurks a warm fuzzy!

Under stress, the influence of drugs or alcohol, or when they are down on themselves, ESTJs are likely to become withdrawn. Alone, they focus on judgments that question their ability, accomplishments or self-worth. Under stress ESTJs may also erupt with hot-tempered, value-laden and destructively personalized judgments of others. They may also find themselves overwhelmed with an emotional attachment to ideals or people. It sometimes manifests itself in what others see as an outburst of fanaticism that lacks the logic or data to support it.

Many of the ESTJ qualities are those that our culture associates with masculinity. Indeed, the word "macho" is an apt one to describe the behavior of many male ESTJs. Myers' research suggests that an unusual proportion of ESTJs may be male. Women who are ESTJs may find themselves caught up in a struggle to maintain their sense of self. Behaviors that are natural expressions of their psychological type may be seen as "inappropriate" for women. They may suffer from subtle and not-so-subtle messages that they should not be what they are.

The growing awareness of the price we all pay for such sex- role stereotyping may have a double benefit. It may help some male ESTJs to recognize that it is not a sign of weakness to be more in touch with their "softer" side. At the same time, it may free some female ESTJs to express the power that is appropriately theirs, too.

ISTJ

ISTJs are private people who take in great quantities of specific, impersonal information. They are likely to remember what others say and do. They are not so likely to be aware of their own emotions, nor are they quick to sense what others are feeling.

When alone they recall specifics about people, places, or things with unusual vividness. It's as if they are constantly taking pictures or movies of what is taking place outside them. They store these pictures inside in such a way that they can retrieve them at any time. They are, therefore, precise and accurate in whatever they say or do.

ISTJs' sense of detail, coupled with a strong need to be organized and orderly, often manifests itself in their homes or apartments. The furniture, fixtures, paintings, and color schemes are both functional and beautiful. They may put much effort and planning into making their homes unusually neat and attractive. They have, though they may not give themselves credit for it, impressive artistic tastes. They like and appreciate beautiful things. And they take care of them.

ISTJs judge the information they take in logically, analytically, and impersonally. They approach things from a practical point of view. They want things to work, to be functional. They have little interest in or tolerance for exotic or impractical ideas or schemes. They are modest and down-to-earth. They apply common sense to whatever they do. Few details get by them. They see the "fine print" perhaps better than any other type.

ISTJs' behavior is governed by shoulds and should nots. They are keenly aware of laws, procedures, traditions, and regulations. They are attracted to careers and occupations where rules and regulations are important. They move into positions that give them opportunities to use their skill with details. They are loyal to the institutions that they are a part of, and they work hard to make them efficient.

In their own lives, ISTJs abide by rules and regulations, and they expect that others will, too. As a result, they may take good work for granted and take notice only of mistakes and errors. They do not often show appreciation in spontaneous ways or give encouragement to others on the spur of the moment. When in leadership positions, they are likely to use the formal rewards system to recognize an employee's outstanding performance. The informal touch is largely lacking unless ISTJs build that into one of their many "shoulds!"

ISTJs are particularly good at following through. They stay with a job until it is complete—in all its painstaking details. They are super-dependable. When they make a commitment, they can be counted on to honor it at all costs. For ISTJs work and obligations come first. Life is a serious business to them. They are not likely to take the time to relax, to goof off, to be lazy. Taking care of themselves comes only after they have met all their obligations. Some ISTJs become workaholics, and as they get older they can pay a heavy price in terms of their health.

ISTJs' sense of responsibility is so great and their dependability so obvious that they are likely to be asked to do more and more. They find if difficult to refuse—or delegate. They get overloaded with work. Their response is to work longer and longer hours. They become trapped and do not know how to get out of it.

They are likely to rise to leadership positions in organizations because they have "paid their dues." They move up one step at a time. They earn each promotion by their perseverance, their hard work and their loyalty to the organization.

They bring stability to organizations. They conserve resources. They do not like to take risks. They weigh decisions carefully against their keen sense of what is realistic. These qualities, combined with their sense of tradition, can make them less than enthusiastic about new ideas or new ways of doing things. On the other hand, when they become convinced that a new approach has practical merit, they will take the necessary steps to see that it works.

ISTJs do not naturally make decisions based on their values. Decisions that convey "I appreciate," "I like," "I want" are not likely to seem valid to them. Focusing on people and how decisions will affect others' feelings is something they do only with effort. When the situation clearly calls for it, when that is something they know they "should" do, they will work hard to do it responsibly and well.

ISTJs' least developed side has to do with the world of possibilities. They are not usually excited by abstract thought. They are not particularly fascinated by complex interrelationships. So great is their concentration on the realities of a situation that they do not often allow themselves to speculate. If situations call for intuitive insights or creative brainstorming, therefore, ISTJs are not likely to be active contributors. They are more likely to see practical possibilities and consequences. And their insights can be penetrating when they can base them on a solid accumulation of relevant data.

When the situation calls for it, some ISTJs take the facts and fit them into "the big picture." They may even enjoy dealing with complex and challenging situations. When theory helps, they learn and apply it in concrete and practical ways. Though never straying far away from practical considerations, they can have a sense of what might be. With those they trust, they may choose to share their visions. If urged to do something about them before they are ready, however, they often pull back and cite practical reasons for not acting. When they are ready to act, their accomplishments are impressive indeed. The combination of a sense of vision with an acute sense of practical realities is rare and powerful. Some ISTJs have it.

More often, however, when ISTJs do look at possibilities, they are likely to think of the most negative ones. Two ISTJs, for example, were once sharing why they hated to travel. Why? All they could focus on was how many things could go wrong on the trip or while they were away! When ISTJs are down on themselves, they often berate themselves for the things they could have done but did not. They will only see possibilities about themselves that have a negative cast. Or they will find themselves in a difficult situation and see no possible way out.

While life is a serious business for ISTJs, many have a lighter side. They can and do sometimes see things from an unexpectedly humorous angle. Their wit is likely to be dry and understated.

One ISTJ was discussing with his work group the qualities required to be effective on the job. Someone said: "Writing skills."

The ISTJ quickly spoke up: "Yes, we have to write good."

"Your grammar is poor," was the quick response.

"You know," said the ISTJ, deadpan, "you're right. My gramma was poor."

Some ISTJs are irrepressibly funny. Others keep their humorous thoughts to themselves. What comes first, however, is their sense of duty and responsibility. ISTJs are pillars of the community and its important institutions. Modest, unassuming, seldom flashy, they themselves may not receive the recognition and appreciation that they have so industriously earned. Take the rest of the day off, ISTJs!

ESFJ

ESFJs are people persons. They like and enjoy people. They meet people easily, and they enjoy situations that give them opportunities to do so. They effortlessly gather specific and detailed information about others. They are endlessly curious about what others do and what is happening to them. They turn all this information into supportive judgments that they share with genuine warmth. As a result, they are frequently very affirming people. They quickly put others at ease and make them feel valued and important.

At a New Year's Eve party, an INTJ took her ESFJ neighbor aside and said: "I have a story to tell you. I have just finished a novel and there is a character in it who has a special gift. Whenever he talks to people, they go away feeling better about themselves. They are not aware of it, but it is because of the things this person has asked them or said to them. When I read the book, I kept thinking, "I know someone who does that." And finally it came to me. It's you. I just wanted to tell you that." The INTJ had captured perfectly one of the best gifts ESFJs have and make so readily available to the world.

ESFJs have a strong sense of responsibility. They are concerned with the details of life. They want to have everything organized and orderly. Thus, they are unusually good at anticipating concrete things that must be done or problems that may arise. They are often able to mobilize themselves or others to insure that what needs to be done does get done. They are, in short, dependable. They follow through on the details of a job or daily living. They enjoy it and are good at it.

They have a high regard for authority—whether the authority of institutions, laws, or people. And they believe that others ought to, too. They can be quick to express shoulds and should nots, which they apply both to themselves and others. They can have a hard time understanding those who do not look at the world in the same way. Those who do not share their views can find ESFJ judgments confining and sometimes sharply critical.

ESFJs are not likely to enjoy the abstract and the theoretical. They prefer that things be kept simple, concrete, and practical. On the other hand, their respect for authority and their regard for people is such that they will make every effort to understand abstract or theoretical subjects, discussions or assignments. This is perhaps particularly true when ESFJs are students.

Like all of us, they want others to "do unto them" what they do so well for others. In short, ESFJs have a high need for affirmation from others. They may need to be told several times that they have done a good job or done the right thing. They may ask for affirmation or approval and express disappointment when it is not forthcoming. And they are quick to sense when affirmation or approval is perfunctorily given.

When ESFJs focus on possibilities, they can find all kinds of things to worry about. Because of their tendency to make quick judgments, they often seem sure that the worst will happen. They become easily afraid and express their doubts and fears in ways that are tiring to others.

When they are depressed or "down on themselves," they often judge themselves impersonally and logically. They become preoccupied with the question: "Did I do the right thing?" And most of the time they are sure they did not. When caught up in these moods, ESFJs reject reassuring responses from others. They sense instantly any hesitation or any qualification on the part of others and see in it a strong negative judgment.

When depressed, they focus their negative thinking on close friends or relatives. They blurt out uncharacteristically cold and harsh judgments of those closest to them. If others fight back, they become deeply hurt. They do not seem to understand that they have brought on the very reaction they now find devastating.

ESFJs are seldom interested in the world of abstract thought. They do not often think about philosophical principles or about basic questions of the meaning of life. It can make them depressed and melancholy, for their conclusions have a negative and depressing quality to them.

ESFJs are more likely to be captured by moody philosophical thinking when alone. To avoid that, they may pick up a book, turn on the radio or television, or—better yet—think of something to do that involves others. And some ESFJs may become devoted members of an established system—religious, social, or political—because it gives them answers. It relieves them of the necessity of having to deal further with what to them are painful questions.

ESFJs warmth, their people orientation, their attention to detail, their sense of responsibility cause them to seek jobs and careers where they can be of service to others. Because they are modest and seldom out for personal place or power, they do not often experience a drive for leadership positions. When they are in leadership positions, their contribution is significant. They work extremely hard to bring about a harmonious working environment. They stabilize an organization. They insure that the tasks are done thoroughly, competently, and on time. In leadership roles, they focus on the here-and-now issues. They are not likely to be either future or change oriented.

In many ways, ESFJs combine many of the best traits that are often associated with women, just as the ESTJ personality seems, of all types, to be the ''macho'' personality. In a world in transition—indeed, one might say turmoil—about such things, this may cause both male and female ESFJs to unnecessarily doubt the powerful strengths they possess.

ISFJ

ISFJs have a particularly rich inner world, which they do not often share with others. When alone, they review the day or an event from an intensely detailed and highly personal perspective. They remember virtually all the specifics, all the facts, all the details of everything that has happened.

They have an amazing capacity to store details. It's as if their minds were videotape cameras that take in everything. Later, they can play and replay the tapes from many different and specific angles.

ISFJs view things literally. They see the facts, and facts are important to them. As a result, they are precise and accurate. They have excellent memories, particularly with regard to people and about things that matter to people.

ISFJs' combination of preferences give them unusual skills as interior decorators, either as amateurs or professionals. Like ISTJs, they have a particularly well developed sense of space, function, and color. Their homes or apartments are often meticulously kept and furnished beautifully. They have excellent artistic judgment.

ISFJs are quiet, gentle, and reflective. They place a high value on people and want to be of service to others. They also place a high value on social institutions that minister to the needs of others. They become important members of those institutions and often become the unsung workers who keep them going. So unassuming are they as they play their roles that they run the risk of being taken for granted.

They share with others their judgments, which are based on the factual data they see and reflect their people orientation. ISFJs respect authority. They accept the traditional values of their family, group, institution or society. They often have trouble understanding those who do not. Capable of quick and firm judgments, ISFJs are likely to temper them by a desire not to hurt others. Also, when alone they revisit their judgments to insure that they have done the fair, proper, and considerate thing.

They are practical, detail-oriented, painstakingly thorough, and exceptionally good at follow through. They and ISTJs are the most duty bound of all types. They are most likely to sacrifice for others or for the job. Relaxation, taking it easy, being lazy—these are all things that ISFJs will allow themselves only after every duty, every obligation is fulfilled.

Because they are so dependable and thorough, ISFJs are often given more and more to do. Their sense of responsibility rarely allows them to say "no." Thus, they can find themselves overburdened, unable to see a way out and not knowing how to ask for help. Their sense of responsibility makes it difficult for them to delegate, which only adds to the work they must do.

ISFJs are often shy. They have a tendency to blend into a group, quietly enjoying what is going on. They do not often feel a need to push themselves into leadership roles. If they do seek such positions, they do not do so aggressively. They work hard and "pay their dues." They earn promotions by their painstaking thoroughness, their mastery of all aspects of the job, their systematic follow through, and their deep commitment to the institution and its mission.

As leaders, they can be counted on to be sensitive to the needs of their staff. They are warm, caring, and nurturing. They are interested in the personal and professional growth of their staffs.

ISFJs are very sensitive to what people are feeling. When they can overcome their reluctance to speak up, they help others to become aware when feelings need to be addressed. As leaders or members of a work group, they know when feelings—their own or others—are affecting group performance and productivity.

They are also unusually aware of their own inner sensations. They know how they are reacting emotionally to what is going on. They don't usually share that knowledge with others. They keep their own feelings bottled up and do not act on them. At times, particularly when they think they have been badly treated, they may build powerful resentments. By not bringing their feelings out in the open and dealing with them, they may get "stuck" emotionally. They may hold rigidly to views of themselves and others that are unnecessary and unproductive.

ISFJs do not naturally make impersonal or analytical judgments. They will push themselves to do so, however, when they think that is what they "should" do or that is how they are expected to act. In doing so, they will feel somewhat uncomfortable and unsure of themselves. It violates their preferred way of making decisions. They prefer to think in terms of people and values.

Their least favored side is the world of possibilities. They will go to considerable lengths to avoid thinking of them. When they do, they are most likely to focus on what can go wrong. They create scenarios that have unhappy endings.

When ISFJs are under stress or down on themselves a negative intuition takes over. They look around them and see only negative possibilities. They become aware, for example, of how much they are taken for granted. In the absence of concrete evidence that others value them, they begin to imagine the worst. They convince themselves that their work is not adequate or that they are not appreciated. Or they convince themselves that they simply cannot get all their work done.

ISFJs may very well share with others their sense of "doom and gloom" about the bad things that are going to happen. They are much less likely to share how they are imagining that others are thinking critical thoughts about them or their work. As they see it, if they have to ask for support or praise, then surely they cannot actually believe what others may say.

In short, ISFJs get discouraged, they put themselves in a no-win situation. Because they are so unassuming, people do, in fact, often take them for granted. They do not get the recognition they deserve, but they won't ask for it, either. When ISFJs get down on themselves, they really get down on themselves! And, in fact, many ISFJs suffer from powerful depressions from which they find it very difficult to extricate themselves.

ISFJs, like ISTJs, often have a very special brand of humor. They take in details and view them from unpredictable and often humorous angles. One young ISFJ watched with his family and friends a fictionalized documentary of a famous murder. When the police led a young woman in handcuffs to jail, the narrator listed her real name, plus several aliases. "Mmm," mused the ISFJ, "it must take her a long time to sign a check!"

ISFJs are generous, giving, helpful, and thoughtful—quietly and unobtrusively so. They sometimes long for others to respond in return and find it difficult to be assertive about that need. They do not sufficiently recognize and give themselves credit for the many good things they do. They see that as doing their duty, not something to take pride in. If ISFJs could add to their list of "shoulds" that they should honor themselves, that they should from time to time ask that the world recognize their many contributions, they might enjoy some of the support and praise they so richly deserve.

III The SP Temperament

Four of the sixteen types (ESTP, ISTP, ESFP, ISFP) share the sensing and perceiving preferences. Of Keirsey's four temperaments, they are the action, activity, competition people. They excel at times of crisis. Keirsey calls them Troubleshooter/Negotiators.

SPs look at the world around them and see facts and realities. They focus on the concrete and the practical. They live in the the here-and-now, the present moment. They want to do things. They have a very high need to feel free to act. To have an impulse and not to be able to follow it is frustrating. They want to keep their options open. They want the flexibility to go with the flow of things. They want to respond to ever-changing here-and-now realities. Action for its own sake excites them.

The need to be active manifests itself in specific, concrete, hands-on activities. And if excitement—risk, even—is involved, so much the better. In times of crisis, their adrenaline goes into high gear, all their senses and energies are mobilized. They are quick, practical, and decisive. They are action-oriented experimenters. They try the first thing that occurs to them. They quickly see whether it works or not. And they are ready just as quickly to try something else if what they have done doesn't work.

They have little ego involved in the actions they take, only the outcome. They have little or no need to defend their actions. They do not need to stick with a course of action to show that it will work or can be made to work. Their sense of accomplishment comes from doing something that will work, from making things happen. Thus, they do not get locked up in rules, regulations or procedures. They do not sit around looking at a situation from all angles, wanting to figure things out before acting.

Just as soon as a crisis is over, SPs are on to something else. They do not dwell on the past, for the past holds no excitement for them. Nor do they dwell on the future, for the future is always too intangible, too far away. The present is what matters, what gives energy, what generates enthusiasm.

One young SP, a college freshman, heard something at the window over her bed one night. She looked up to see a peeping Tom. By the next morning, she had talked to the other girls in her off-campus dorm and found that others had had similar experiences. That same morning, she got all the girls together in her room to discuss what to do.

When the group seemed to her to be talking in circles, the SP said clearly and firmly: "I think we ought to call the police."

When no immediate consensus developed, she said, "I am going to call the police," and she did.

The policeman who came shortly thereafter took the girls' story. He looked at them and said, "Well, if beautiful young girls like you don't draw the shades, what do you expect?"

That did it. The SP girl, knowing her mother worked as a human services information specialist in another state, got on the phone again. Quickly she learned about the proper authorities to contact. Then she called her father to see if she could get further information. She listened attentively to him as long as he stayed in the here-and-now. But as soon as he began to think ahead, she cut him off.

By noon she had contacted a Rape Prevention Center, a state legislator, and college authorities. By mid-afternoon, the police chief, a representative of the state legislator, and a lawyer from the Rape Prevention Center met with the girls. Apologies were made for the officer's inappropriate remarks. The girls were given useful information and assured of instant help should they need it. There were no further peeping Tom incidents.

For the SP, the crisis brought out instant leadership, decisive action, and a remarkable maturity for an 18-year-old. The moment it was over, it was over. She never made reference to the incident again. She did not dwell on it, talk about it, relive it to recreate the drama and the excitement. It was over. The here-and-now drew her attention and energy.

SPs, despite their focus on facts and realities, are not always concerned about being accurate when they discuss or cite specifics. When discussing past situations, in fact, they may make up facts and not be at all concerned if confronted with their errors. Why? The center of their attention is intensely focused on the specifics of the here-and-now. As soon as a here-and-now becomes a there-and-then, the specifics have lost their relevance. SPs' observational strength and accuracy relates to the specifics of the immediate present, to what is taking place in the world around them at the moment.

Theirs is not the world of the theoretical or the abstract. Fantasy seldom has any appeal for them. Unless they can see some practical and—preferably—immediate relevance to information or knowledge, they are likely to get bored, impatient and frustrated. Knowing something for the sake of knowing it means little to SPs, who may be the most literal-minded of the eight sensing types. They are so focused on the concrete that they find it more difficult than others to see patterns in problems or situations and to generalize from those patterns. They see each new problem or situation as unique, and even the smallest of interconnections, unless made clear to them, are likely to pass them by.

SPs and the World of Work

SPs who rise to leadership positions generally do so under conditions that call for their particular strengths. They like jobs that involve handling the unexpected, that require dealing with constant crises or upheaval, that demand flexibility or the ability to negotiate difficult situations. They are hands-on managers. They are always where the action is. They concentrate on immediate problems. They are quick and ingenious in solving them.

SP managers are not likely to be interested in long-range planning or policy formulation. They don't pay homage to established rules and regulations, particularly in crisis situations. Writing memorandums and position papers holds little or no appeal for them. Nor do extended staff meetings. These things only delay getting things done.

More often than not, there is a sense of excitement wherever SP managers are, for they are usually involved in crises. In times of calm, SP managers become bored. Many of them will admit that they look for a crisis so that they will have something interesting to do. A few will admit to creating one, if necessary, to liven up their work. SPs' skills in pressured and difficult situations explain Keirsey's Troubleshooter/Negotiator name for them.

Consultant Ichak Adizes identifies four types of managers he has found in his work. One in particular sounds much like Keirsey's SP temperament. Adizes sees some managers as focused on producing immediate results. They are always in the midst of crises, doing things themselves. They need what he calls "expediters" or "go-fors" around them. When operating effectively, he calls these managers "Producers." They are producers of results. They excel at getting things done. They tend to be compulsively busy. They live for the moment.

When not operating effectively, he calls them "Lone Rangers" or "Fire Fighters." He suggests that they try to do too much themselves. They do not delegate responsibility. They do not plan. They pay little attention to coordinating or following through. Adizes' Lone Rangers or Fire Fighters have characteristics that are remarkably similar to those that ineffectual SPs share, just as Producers have many of the same qualities of successful SP managers and leaders.

The sense of excitement SP managers can generate when "pulling the fat out of the fire" gives them a certain charisma—particularly for young people. Theirs is a "crisis charisma." They have unique abilities to galvanize people's attention, energy and emotions in difficult or dangerous situations. They are very loyal to those who are loyal to them. They have a difficult time understanding those who do not appreciate the "edge of disaster" that they seem to thrive on. They don't understand those who long for things to "settle down" so that they can get "back" to a "normal" work "routine."

"I've finally recognized," said one SP secretary, "that I'll probably never stay in one position very long. I'm attracted to a new position for the excitement, the newness of it. I usually find a mess, plunge right into it, straighten it out, and then get bored. Maintaining things is no fun."

"Being a therapist," said one SP manager of a hotline counseling center, "never appealed to me. What I do here does."

"I need help," one SP manager told a consultant. "Either my managers need an attitude transplant, or I do." Not one of his subordinate managers was an SP. All were frustrated at his frenetic work style. They saw him as doing nothing to stop the constant crises inundating the organization. On the other hand, the "kiddie corps"—the bright, energetic young staff whose help he often enlisted, ignoring the chain-of-command—were devoted to him, as he was to them. SP managers over time select for subordinate managerial positions those staff who enjoy their leadership style. Or they build a "kitchen cabinet" of supportive managers and staff.

As might be expected, many SPs emerge as leaders or managers in times of crises. In wartime, for example, SPs often get battlefield promotions. Or SPs may be asked to take over troubled organizations to get production rolling again. SPs are also likely to gravitate toward those positions within professions where there is continual variety, crisis, tension or danger. SPs who enter the medical profession, for example, are most likely to go either into general practice in towns or medium-size cities or into surgery or into emergency room practice. Some become Presidents of the United States! There is considerable evidence that Andrew Jackson, Theodore Roosevelt and Ronald Reagan share the SP temperament.

SP Children and Students

SPs often become disenchanted with school beginning sometime in junior high. Because they love action, because they are not theoretically inclined, school makes less and less sense to them. The higher the grade level, the more theoretical and abstract the curriculum gets. Some SPs manage to put up with it. Others, unable to control their need for physical action, begin to behave in ways that teachers see as disruptive. Indeed, one counselor tried to convince the mother of an ESTP whose IQ was clearly in the gifted range that her son was "brain-damaged!"

Teachers, in fact, often misinterpret SPs' behavior. They don't recognize it for what it is. They do not accept as legitimate the SP need for action and activity. Teachers do not understand that SPs are disinterested in conceptual or abstract things unless they see direct or immediate value. Instead, many teachers think there is something wrong or lacking in SP students.

"This child," wrote one NT chemistry teacher about an SP student, "need to develop her logical and critical thinking."

It would never have occurred to this teacher to say to herself: "With this child, I need to be particularly careful to show how each concrete piece links together with the next concrete piece. I will do better if I have her learn chemistry by doing it—in the lab, with experiments."

Is it any wonder, then, that SPs are education's casualties? Is it any wonder that they drop out of school in greater numbers than other temperaments? Is it any wonder that they are more likely to exhibit "behavior" problems and get into trouble with school and other authorities?

SPs are as bright as their friends. They can learn abstract or theoretical things. What they need is a curriculum that allows for learning-by-doing. They need options that allow for independent or group projects involving action or physical activity. They need convincing that there is practical usefulness in what they are studying. Is that too much to ask?

In the absence of a supportive home or school environment, many SPs begin to underestimate themselves. In some it can be seen directly. Others try to mask it with a mixture of seeming indifference, arrogance, or bravado. Many drop out of school or discontinue their educations after high school. Those who do continue are likely to either take technical or professional training. Those who take the more traditional liberal arts curriculum are likely to be motivated by some technical or professional career that requires a liberal arts degree. Of all the SPs, the ISTP is most likely to be able to cope effectively with traditional curricula and traditional teaching strategies.

Many SPs have an untraditional path through higher education. They don't begin when their friends do. They may go a year or so and drop out, only to re-enroll when their life experiences make further education relevant to them. For many, a key is being convinced that their educations will lead to something useful, practical, profitable—to something they value.

SPs take special understanding, because traditional ways of doing things and traditional educational experiences do not fit them. Trying to force them into traditional ways is not likely to work. Their need to be active, to be doing things, may cause them to exhibit rebellious behavior.

A father watched how his SP daughter spent a weekend picking up her room, which most often looked like a cyclone had hit it. Noticing how quickly it became a mess again, he said to her: "You spend so much time picking up your room. Then just getting dressed to go to school in the morning, you mess it up. Why don't you hang things up when you take them off? Wouldn't it be much easier to keep your room clean once you've spent all that time picking things up?"

Said the SP daughter to her NT father: "Oh Daddy, I've tried it your way. It only cramps my style!"

An unusually sensitive type-knowledgeable high school teacher watched his two SP students closely. When he saw that they would not be able to sit still much longer, he devised stategies like:

"Bill, why don't you get up, go to the board, draw a sketch of what's going on right now and explain it to us?"

"Or, he might simply say, "Roger, go take a walk for five minutes and come back before you burst."

The combination of sensing and perceiving gives many SPs unusual skills at anything that involves eye-hand coordination. Some are gifted athletes, musicians, performers, artists and craftsmen. Some become aware of their gifts. Others—having come to underestimate themselves because they seem out of step with school, their parents, or their brothers and sisters—never fully appreciate the gifts they have.

A Final Word

SP adults are likely to be lively and fun to be around. Be prepared to enjoy the unexpected, to do things spontaneously, to deal with impulsive suggestions. Don't be thrown off by promises or commitments not met.

SPs are full of projects. Some they see through to completion. Many they carry up to a point and then drop for something else. SP adults if they get down on themselves can become immobilized from doing the very thing that can restore their sense of confidence—throwing themselves into some activity. For it is in the activity itself that SPs define themselves. It is through the activity that they work out issues and problems. It is through action, activity and competition that they find fulfillment and make their best contributions.

ESTP

ESTPs are outgoing, straight-talking, straight-shooting types with a flair for the dramatic. They constantly scan the environment and take in detailed observations about people and activities. They notice many fine points in the world around them that escape the notice of others. They focus their attention on practical things, on impersonal facts and realities. They have an endless appetite for concrete and useful information.

They live very much in the present. They are oriented to the "here-and-now" and are into the activity of the moment. Neither the past nor the future have much claim on the attention of ESTPs. They are enthusiastic and adventuresome. They dive right into the middle of whatever is going on, always willing to explore new things or new ways of doing things. They are quick to size up a situation and pragmatic in the ways they react to it. ESTPs are not observers, they are doers.

ESTPs make crisp, logical, and impersonal decisions about the facts. They look at what works and what doesn't work. They decide quickly what should be done, execute their decisions, and move on to the next exciting thing to do. They do not dwell on decisions. They are not likely to be reflective. "Do it and get on with it." That is the characteristic way for ESTPs.

ESTPs do not mince words. They are blunt and to-the-point. They are particularly good in crisis situations. Their willingness to plunge right in, to get their hands dirty, to take risks, to experiment, to try a variety of things, to go for the quick and expedient solution to the problem at hand makes them unusually effective in crises.

When working things out, ESTPs have scant regard for existing rules, regulations, or procedures. Making something work is what's paramount in their approach. If things can be done within the rules, fine. If not, do what needs to be done anyway and worry about the rules afterwards. "Never go to a lawyer," said one ESTP administrator, "until you know what answer you want. Then be sure to phrase the question so that you get the answer you want."

This is not to say that ESTPs lack integrity—far from it. ESTPs tend to have a bottom line past which they will not go, and they will sacrifice their careers before they will do what they know to be wrong. One career civil servant was written up in *Washingtonian* magazine one year as the "toughest bureaucrat in Washington." The next year, the Secretary of his Department is reported to have told the White House: "Get rid of him. Either he goes or I go." The ESTP is no longer there.

Without something exciting to focus on, without an outlet for their energies and abilities, ESTPs are likely to get bored. They need to do things. They prefer variety and a fast pace. They generally radiate excitement and energy with whatever they do. They love fun, are impulsive, often electric personalities. They have a sense for the dramatic, are excellent at improvising. They excel at making things up as they go along. They are risk-takers, sometimes gamblers. They can "hustle" almost any situation or anybody. They enjoy being the center of attention and often are. They enjoy the good life and often know where the good things are.

Despite the ability that ESTPs have to size up situations and people, they are not always aware of the emotional impact of their behavior on others. If they are aware, they may not care—unless it makes a difference in something they want to achieve. They do not often make decisions that are person-centered or based on a process of sorting out what values ought to govern in a given situation.

ESTPs are often impatient with theory—unless they can see immediate, practical applications. They seldom stay with a theory long enough to test whether it might, in fact, be useful or not. They can also get impatient with those who speak in terms of possibilities. They often see possibilities as the product of impractical fantasy or a wild imagination. Their own hunches generally are unpleasant ones. They don't trust their own hunches or those of others. On rare occasions, some ESTPs have sweeping flashes of insight—sometimes creative and positive, sometimes dangerously off base. Some ESTPs find an outlet for their intuition by reading science-fiction novels or other kinds of novels that deal with the mystic or mysterious.

ESTPs often have trouble in school. Sometimes their need for activity is misunderstood. Sometimes they act out their disinterest in subject matters that they can see no practical use for. The more bored they get, the more they may act out in ways that are disruptive. Teachers then see them as discipline problems. They don't know what to do with ESTPs who are bright but whose behavior and performance do not reflect their intellectual ability. One counselor actually labeled a young ESTP of "genius" IQ as "brain damaged." He put pressure on the boy's mother to put him into vocational programs!

When ESTPs are down on themselves, they are likely to withdraw into themselves and focus on negative possibilities. They become moody and focus their negative possibilities on themselves. They underrate themselves. They may paralyze themselves instead of getting involved and doing something, which is the source of their greatest strength.

When depressed, they often spend too much time alone. They withdraw from contact with others. They end up becoming depressed and getting stuck in moods of helplessness and self-pity. They may not choose to share their inner struggle with others, even close friends. They may, instead, simply become irritable and short-tempered when asked why they are not being their usual ebullient selves.

Freedom-loving, energetic, unpredictable, gifted at handling difficult and tense situations, ESTPs need to avoid being tied down to constraining jobs and assignments that allow no outlet for their abilities. To get the most from ESTPs, give them the challenge they need, the running room to show what they can do, and recognize that the mundane and the routine are not for them.

ISTP

ISTPs have a compelling drive to analyze the inner working of things that interest them. They want to understand what makes things "tick." They focus their powers of logical analysis on concrete and practical subjects. Unless they can see a practical application, they are not interested. They tear apart machines to see what makes them work. They use their knowledge of psychological type to conduct statistical studies on marriage patterns.

They do their best thinking when alone, for that's when they find it easiest to sort things out. That is when they form clear, logical judgments about whatever piques their curiosity.

With others, they talk about information—information about specific, tangible things. They absorb impersonal facts in large quantities. They are happiest when they can go off by themselves and make judgments about those facts. They put them into a logical framework and figure out what categories will best explain things. ISTPs can thus be excellent statisticians or statistical researchers. When working with a project that appeals to them, they seek clarity and logical consistency. They will work hard to tie up any loose ends.

While ISTPs can be at home in a theoretical world, they are not abstract conceptualizers, nor are they interested in speculative thinking. For ISTPs to get involved in theory, they must be able to see its practical value. They must be able to see something useful in it. The focus of their energies is making things work. ISTPs can, in fact, get very impatient with theories they view as having no immediate, practical value. They do not often understand types (like INTJs and INTPs) who seem to them to love theory for the sake of theory. Why would anyone want to look at, study, and dissect things from a purely skeptical point of view? Who cares how many angels there are on the head of a pin?

In their outer lives, ISTPs are flexible, spontaneous, and adaptable. They focus on the here-and-now. They are interested in details. They want to know about practical and pragmatic things. They are quick, decisive, logical, and impersonal. Of all the SP temperaments, they are the least likely to find themselves out of step with school. Their introversion and ability to think logically helps. It gives them interest, skills and—probably most important—some of the patience to put up with subject matter and teaching methods that place a severe strain on other SPs.

ISTPs, like other SPs, are often gifted with good eye-hand coordination and thus may excel at sports and other physical activities. If interested in sports, ISTPs may remember team schedules, game scores, and all kinds of team and individual records. Many ISTPs are fascinated with tools. They enjoy working with them and are very good at it. One ISTP admitted that when he could not figure out how something worked, he waited until it had served its usefulness. Then, if he could do it no other way, he would saw it in half just to be able to satisfy his curiosity.

ISTPs are action oriented. They respond to what is immediately before them. They often have superb technical skills and are effective technical leaders, especially in crisis situations. They want to be up and about, moving around, interacting with machines, equipment, and people. They are not interested in long range planning or scheduling. Setting up policies and procedures and following them does not engage their attention or energies.

The intuitive side of ISTPs is relatively undeveloped. If they make effective intuitive leaps, it will be because they have built a solid foundation of specific facts. On the other hand, they can have an appreciation for those who are at home in the world of possibilities. Some ISTPs enjoy taking the intuitive insights of others and testing them to see if they hold up under the facts. They use their powers of logical analysis to discover potential usefulness.

ISTPs avoid making judgments based on values. They are not naturally sensitive to people and their emotions. They are so caught up in collecting and analyzing impersonal details that they are not likely to be aware of how they are affecting others. They distrust their own emotions, have trouble distinguishing emotional reactions from value judgments, and make every attempt to ignore or suppress that side of their personalities.

When the pressures of life get too great, however, they may explode in a bad-tempered outburst. That only reinforces their belief that they should keep better control of themselves. They may also go to the other extreme. They can become overwhelmed with feelings of sentimentality or lost in infatuations and feel compelled to share them with others—whether it is appropriate to do so or not. When ISTPs get down on themselves, they are likely to express negative value judgments about themselves. They can, for example, define their self-worth by their ability—usually their inability—to perform some external task. They will then approach these tasks with grim emotional tension, expecting the worst.

ISTPs combination of preferences makes them, like INTPs, unusually shy, particularly in the beginning of relationships. They may find it difficult to take those kinds of extraverted actions that would bring to the attention of others the powerful strengths they have. Unless a crisis galvanizes them into action or unless they are dealing with a subject that deeply interests them, they may unnecessarily hold back and keep to themselves insights that others would find helpful. If they will push themselves a little more into the extraverted world, others will benefit from their abilities and they will find life more fulfilling.

ESFP

ESFPs focus their energies on collecting concrete information about the world around them, particularly about people. They are outgoing, friendly, sociable, and party-loving. They are alert to and consistently interested in what is going on at the moment with friends, acquaintances, or fellow workers. They love to socialize.

ESFPs are very much here-and-now people. They are are keenly aware of exactly what is happening at the moment. In some ways, they are like a movie camera that is sweeping over the world around them. They focus mainly on specific, detailed information about people in that external landscape. That is how they view the world, and that is the world they love to be a part of.

ESFPs are practical and down-to-earth people. They are not prone to a lot of speculation about what might have been or what might be. They are too busy with what is. They are too busy enjoying themselves. They are too busy playing at work, working at play, and having fun doing it all.

ESFPs most often keep their judgments to themselves. When alone, they sort things out. They make decisions about what and whom they value. What others most often see is the easy warmth and sociability, the generous support and empathy. ESFPs don't like to be critical or judgmental.

Life is best for ESFPs when it is fun. They are attracted to whatever is light and happy. They avoid or find boring situations that are serious, heavy, theoretical or speculative. They like to help people in specific and concrete ways. Helping to bring pleasure to others gives ESFPs a sense of satisfaction. They like helping others solve immediate, hands on problems.

ESFPs love variety and action. They like to make things happen. Many of them enjoy jobs that involve selling things to people. Their outgoing natures, their focus on the concrete, their appreciation of people, their flexibility and spontaneity, and their "gift of gab" all contribute to their ability to be very successful in sales work or any line of work that involves persuasion—including politics!

ESFPs are performers. Many of them, particularly males, for example, are attracted to athletics. Sports activities appeal to their enjoyment of action, activity and competition. Many of them are gifted athletically. Others develop their skills by their determination, energy and enthusiasm. Still others try acting or other performing arts. Others get into music. Being active, being with others, is what makes these things appealing to ESFPs.

ESFPs enjoy moving into chaotic situations. They will get things done. They will bring order out of chaos. But don't ask them to stay around and maintain things in an organized and orderly fashion. ESFPs will be bored to death, and they may create a little crisis just to have something exciting to do. ESFPs whose work does not provide enough variety and action may move from one job to another. As soon as a job becomes routine, they may leave.

ESFPs can suffer from being too impulsive. They are not the best judges of the time it will take to complete a task. They procrastinate before starting something important, particularly if it does not appeal to them, and end up working overtime to make a deadline.

It is difficult for ESFPs to be objective and impersonal in making decisions. They can do it, but it makes them uneasy. It violates their need to be warm, supportive and friendly. The least developed side of ESFPs is the world of the speculative, the abstract, the theoretical. They have little or no patience with anything that doesn't deal with reality. It's all idle speculation to them.

When they must deal with possibilities they are likely to go to extremes. They will either think of possibilities so unrealistic, so ungrounded, as to be pure wish-fulfilling fantasy. Or they may go to the depths of doom and gloom, see despair everywhere and no possible way out. Because of their tendency to get lost in negative possibilities, ESFPs have difficulty dealing with their own anxieties. They do their best, therefore, to ignore looking at situations that may be troublesome. They prefer to put a bright face on things, to pretend that everything is OK.

When under stress or down on themselves, ESFPs become captured by what is their least developed side—intuition. The focus of their attention shifts from the world outside them inward to themselves. They pay little attention to specifics, to facts about themselves. Instead, they begin to ask questions about the meaning and direction of their own lives. In short, ESFPs withdraw from their friends and associates and ruminate on negative possibilities about themselves. They see themselves caught up in lose-lose situations with no way out. They see possibilities—exciting futures—for others but not for themselves.

For the most part, however, ESFPs are fun to be with. They add sparkle, excitement, and cheer wherever they go. They exude warmth and sympathy. They can make things happen. They make things work. Their zest for living is contagious. They draw others into their fun-loving, often prankish, activities.

Too many ESFPs shortchange themselves. They think less highly of themselves than they should. Formal education is often a major contributor to ESFPs' tendency to doubt themselves. With each grade, school becomes more abstract and more theoretical and less activity and action oriented. In short, the curriculum and traditional teaching methods do not meet the needs of many ESFPs.

If ESFPs will recognize that there may be nothing wrong with them, that it is the environment that is out of step, they may be more likely to develop and maintain the positive self-image they deserve. A little arrogance for ESFPs, please!

ISFP

To those who do not know them well, ISFPs can seem light-hearted and carefree, and, indeed, they often are. Out of sight from most people, however, they are driven by deeply-held values or by a search for them. Personal values guide their lives. The process of identifying and clarifying what matters to them is serious and important work. To see them, as some do, simply as "free spirits" is to overlook their inner depth and complexity.

ISFPs gather a wealth of specific information about people. They constantly seek to discover what the information means. As a result, often from an early age, they have an unusual degree of empathy. They are frequently penetratingly accurate in their judgments of others.

These gifts, together with their concern for others, give them powerful skills as counselors or therapists. Probably more of them would enter these fields if there were training programs that met their needs. They learn best through action, variety, and hands-on experience. They find the learning of abstract theory either difficult or boring.

ISFPs are intensely practical and very much here-and-now people. They are at their best when they see life as an adventure. They can be fearless in tackling complex or complicated tasks of an immediate, practical, or manual nature. They absorb easily and quickly many details, see possible sources of action, and move quickly to bring about a desired result.

ISFPs are action-oriented, hands-on problem solvers. Their style is warm, sympathetic, and people-oriented. In the service of people, they can cut through a tangle of airline fares to get the cheapest flight. They can be superb crisis or hot-line counselors. They can solve the intricacies of bureaucratic red tape standing in the way of a personnel action. And they can do it all with a flair—albeit a quiet one. They often make what they do seem effortless.

ISFPs love action. They want to be doing things. They are turned off by the esoteric and theoretical. They don't respond well to traditionally oriented curriculums that place heavy emphasis on the development of abstract thinking and critical analysis. Before they can become invested in education, they need to see its practical value. They need to know in concrete terms what use it will have for them in their lives.

They need the space and freedom to find their own way in the world. The usual paths of life are often not for them. Finding their own way is often painful and difficult because they have a deep desire to please. It is altogether too easy for them to lose their sense of self-worth, to find themselves caught in a quiet, often unseen struggle to hang on to a positive self-image.

ISFPs are not particularly at home in the world of possibilities. They may enjoy the intuitive insights of others so long as they can see the practical applications. It is more difficult for them to appreciate the world of the impersonal, the logical, for that is their least developed side. When depressed or down on themselves, however, they rigidly and impersonally judge themselves—or others—against the very standards they normally have no patience with.

ISFPs can also be critical of others—surprisingly so, given their outwardly happy-go-lucky appearance. They are very quick to pick up on specific behaviors. They are unusually aware of what others are doing and thinking. They immediately judge all the specifics they see in a highly subjective and value-oriented way. And sometimes those judgments are harsh indeed. ISFPs, particularly if they are unhappy, may then try to use logic to support their conclusion.

Thus, for example, they can be aware of some nuance in someone else's behavior and instantly find it displeasing. And then the logical conclusion locks in with an unreasoning finality: "That person just did a mean thing to me. They don't like me. I am going to get back at them." Or they may focus more on their own behavior: "My brother has just said he wants to take me on a three-day cycling trip for my birthday [the specific]. I don't want to do that (the value judgment). If I tell him, I'll hurt his feelings (the "logical" conclusion). Oh, what am I going to do (now locked into a lose-lose situation)."

ISFPs who get caught up in their least developed side tend to have a great deal of anger. They will direct logical and angry judgments at themselves or others. Some deal with their anger by withdrawing—sometimes sullenly—from relationships. Some may "act out" their anger by "getting back at" those whom they believe have "picked on them." Some may get into self-punishing or self-destructive behaviors. And some hold on to their anger, cycling through specific episodes over and over again, either in their own minds or with someone they trust.

As a result of their combination of preferences, many ISFPs have an almost constant struggle to believe in themselves. They find it difficult to develop and nourish a strong sense of self-worth. They do not give themselves enough credit for their accomplishments. They see in others' behaviors negative messages that are not there. Because they often have trouble being assertive, they run the risk of getting "stuck" in behaviors and feelings that are not productive for them.

Underneath that carefree exterior, that ease with the here- and-now, ISFPs are truly "still waters that run deep." ISFPs will find that it can pay rich dividends to learn how to be effectively assertive. They need, sometimes, to push themselves to the forefront, to be the center of attention. They need to see in themselves what others so often see in them: How lively they are. How exciting their zest for freedom and spontaneity is. How powerful is their grace under pressure. How in their own quiet ways, they are competently and often confidently making valuable contributions, particularly in people-related tasks or careers that reflect their deeply held personal values.

IV The NT Temperament

Four types—ENTJ, INTJ, ENTP, INTP—comprise one of Keirsey's four temperament groupings. Keirsey calls them Visionaries. He describes them as architects—architects of change, buildings, or theories.

These four types share preferences for intuition and thinking. Intuition helps them see possibilities. They look for meanings and relationships. They like to think about ideas and abstractions, concepts and theories, buildings and organizations. Their insights have an impersonal quality.

NTs also share a preference for making logical and analytical judgments. They subject their intuitive insights to impersonal analysis. They judge data by examining logical consequences and weighing cause-and-effect. They look to abstract principles to guide them in their decision-making.

The combination of intuition and thinking gives NTs a life-long drive—in some it amounts to an obsession—with competence. Intuition sees what competence (or excellence) looks like. Thinking decides "if it's worth doing, it's worth doing well."

NTs' desire to be competent at anything they do profoundly affects their behavior. Some NTs can become fiercely competitive, because that is how they demonstrate to their own satisfaction that they are competent. Some lose interest in something as soon as they have become good at it. For others, the interest is life-long. They constantly seek ways to improve or expand their range of abilities. And some NTs will not undertake an activity if they think they cannot be good at it.

"I don't understand," said an NF to an NT. "My tai chi instructor has said you could join us for my lesson today. Rad's going to. Why don't you?"

"You don't understand," said the NT to the NF. "Tai chi looks very interesting to me, and I think it would also be good for me. But I know myself well enough to know that if I got started, I would want to be good at it. I suspect that to be good at tai chi takes a real investment of time. I don't have room in my life now for all the things I'm already doing . . . Sorry, but I'm not going to tempt myself."

Though he knew it would be fun to join in on the lesson, the NT would not do so. The price he might have paid for a little fun was to get hooked, and he knew what that meant!

The combination of intuition and thinking gives NTs a long-range and frequently sweeping view of things. Hence Keirsey's term "Visionaries" for NTs. The "big picture" focus comes naturally to them. In fact, they need to know the "context" of any issue or problem before they can begin to think constructively about it.

They have a marked tendency to take any issue and view it from different and ever larger or more complex perspectives. As they do so, they can get more and more enthusiastic about the possibilities. As one NF has put it, intuitives "jump lily pads." That can leave others, particularly sensing types, wondering how "we got there from here." In fact, some get so lost in exploring the context of an issue that they sometimes forget what the issue was in the first place!

NTs are very much at home in the world of ideas, theories and abstractions. They enjoy working with them, developing and refining them, adapting and applying them. They can often discern the underlying dynamics of a problem or situation. They are excellent conceptualizers. They can grasp quickly complex situations, see interconnections, analyze implications, and identify alternative solutions.

NTs want to know "why" and "why not." They want to have things make logical sense. They are forever questioning why things are the way they are, challenging assumptions, traditions, habits and customs. NTs, in short, are change oriented. Keirsey calls NTs "architects of change." Seeing new things to do or new ways of doing things is second nature to them.

For NTPs, the excitement is in identifying and developing the blueprint for change. For NTJs, there is satisfaction in following through. They want to be sure that the change actually takes place. NTPs would rather leave the implementation to others. Neither of them, however, have a great deal of patience for the detailed aspects of implementation. Those tasks, all NTs would rather leave to others!

When they think of doing something new, they do not want to hear that it cannot be done. They do not want to hear statements like: "What do you want to do that for? What's the matter with the way we've always done it?" A political slogan from the early 19th century would not appeal at all to NTs:

"Be not the first by whom the new is tried,
"Nor yet the last to lay the old aside."

That sentiment might appeal to SJs, but not to NTs. Indeed, given their differences with regard to stability and change, NTs and SJs frequently have problems understanding and working well together.

NTs often have trouble with authority, whether the authority of place or position. "You've been told," a grizzled, many-times decorated Master Sergeant told a group of young soldiers in a lecture on military courtesy, "that you salute the bars, not the man. As far as I'm concerned, that's nonsense. When I see an officer, I expect him to prove to me he's competent to be one. He's got to prove to me that I owe him the courtesy of a salute." That's a typical NT sentiment with regard to authority, for NTs tend to judge others the same way they judge themselves. Competence is the all-important criteria.

Degrees, pedigrees, rank, position—all these things mean little to most NTs. When they see competence, that is another matter. They can be unusually respectful— deferential, even—to those they see as competent. Authority and competence are two ways of saying the same thing to most NTs. Like the old sergeant, conventional definitions of authority mean little to them.

NTs are not particularly sensitive to people's feelings. They are largely unaware of other's emotions. It's not that they don't care about people or want to work effectively with them. Many, in fact, devote their lives to teaching, managing, or helping people. They can be good at it. Their focus, however, is on the content or the task, not on people's feelings. NTs see possibilities in what people say and do. NTs connect content with people. NTs hear the "what" more than the "who." They decide what fits and what doesn't. They determine what is true or not true. And they "tell it like it is," largely unaware— sometimes unconcerned—that they may have hurt or angered someone in the process.

NT teachers, for example, concentrate on how to get the content across to their students. They want to get students excited about what they are teaching. They don't pay as much attention to what their students may want or need. NTs who conduct workshops may not be aware that they have overloaded participants with content. They may not recognize that participants need a coffee break!

NTs are impersonal visionaries. In higher education, for example, NTs might develop a blueprint for what a meaningful liberal arts education should look like. They know how it can enrich the lives of students. What excites them is not so much the students themselves as what a good education can do for students.

NTs and the World of Work

As managers, NTs may decide that productivity will take care of itself if employees are carefully selected, treated well, and have a stake in the corporation. If that is their driving vision, NT managers will devote a great deal of time and attention to people issues. What is the central focus, however, is the corporation. People are the means to an end.

Like other temperaments, NTs like leadership positions that draw upon their strengths. NTs are good at roles that require providing a new sense of direction. They have the skills to help organizations that are undergoing change or turmoil. NT leaders see new ventures to get involved in, new programs to develop, new organizational structures to design, or new buildings to erect. NT leaders can galvanize staff, mobilize energies, and create dramatic and long-lasting change. NT leaders have their own brand of charisma—idea charisma. The powerful and articulate expression of a new vision is the source of their greatest strength. There is considerable evidence that Presidents Woodrow Wilson and John F. Kennedy were NTs.

NTs measure others against their high standards of competence. They can, sometimes without knowing it, be very clear about who they believe is worthy of their confidence and who is not. They can ignore an organizational chain-of-command and draw around them an insiders' group of bright and ambitious staff members.

NTs, in fact, are often seen as elitists. One NT, a high-ranking government official, stated his position bluntly: "I have only so much time and I can't waste it. I look around me and I see which of my managers and staff are casualties and which are not. I don't waste my time with casualties." Many NT managers are more balanced and devote time, energy and patience to developing their staffs. They do so more enthusiastically, however, when impressed with the intellectual abilities, the mental quickness, the range and vision of their subordinates.

NT managers sometimes get into trouble when they question the competence of their colleagues or their bosses. They too often show their impatience or their contempt. They can become quick, brusque, or challenging in their interactions with others. NTJs, in particular, can be so intimidating that staff are afraid to stand up to them on important issues. Alienated staff may deliberately withhold information and watch with pleasure while the NTJs dig their own graves.

NT leaders and managers can sometimes overdo change. Some like change just for the sake of change. They may have little regard for its impact on the organization. They are often risk-takers. Effective NTs know when, where and how to take risks. They do so only when convinced that their actions will increase profits, improve productivity, or achieve other desirable organizational goals. Other NTs needlessly risk themselves and their organizations in ill-advised ventures.

Management consultant Ichak Adizes in *How to Solve the Mismanagement Crisis* uses two apt words to describe NT managers. They can be the organization's Entrepreneurs or its Arsonists. Entrepreneurs generate vital new ideas. They see profitable opportunities and know how to go after them. They excite others with their creativity and risk-taking. Arsonists are Entrepreneurs run amok. Arsonists light new fires every day. They have more pet projects than the organization has resources to implement. They get incredibly excited about a new direction. They initiate a flurry of activity, then forget it or lose interest. Tomorrow they come up with another new project, and the process repeats itself. Adizes' Entrepreneurs/Arsonists sound very much like Keirsey's NTs.

NT Children and Students

NT children and students are endlessly curious, often challenging, and very sensitive to being treated unfairly or unjustly. The fewer the rules the better, as far as they are concerned, and, please, let those few rules make sense. "A rule is a rule is a rule" is nonsense to them. NT children and students are likely to want the independence both at home and in school to do things their way. They may not appreciate a parent or teacher who wants detailed information. When asked what was it about his SJ mother that caused his ill-temper, the young NT responded angrily, "her questions only slow me down!"

At a young age, NT students begin to make judgments about the competence of their teachers. They work extremely hard for those teachers whom they respect. If they challenge teachers they respect, they do it in an earnest effort to learn or in such a way as to convey their basic good will. When NT students decide that a teacher is not up to their standards, however, they can become disruptively challenging. They turn their energies to asking questions to embarrass the teacher. They are likely to do less than their best in classes with teachers they do not respect.

NTs begin to make decisions relatively early about which courses or subjects are worth their best efforts. They can be blunt to the point of being obnoxious when stating their opinions about courses or subjects they do not like. "I view learning both critically and enthusiastically," wrote one NT high school senior of himself. "One teacher may feel I'm arrogant and aloof while another values my lively participation and polite attentiveness."

NT Adults and Parents

As mates or in adult relationships, NTs place a high value on intellectual companionship. They also have a sentimental side, often one that seems mushy and unpredictable to others. With spouses or close friends, NTs let their guards down. They feel free to explore all the "far-out" things they cannot safely say elsewhere. If with other NTs, one idea often sparks another, and soon the air can be electric with the exchange of thoughts and insights. To other temperaments, all this intellectual "stuff" can get tiring. For other temperaments life is more than theories, strategies, conceptualizing, thinking "big"—and talking about it.

NTs, however caring and thoughtful they may be, are often unaware of the emotional state of family or friends. Or, if aware, they may not know how to deal with emotional issues. In their confusion, they ignore them if at all possible. One NT whenever he saw his wife upset or sick thought to cheer her up by cooking a special and expensive meal. It took him three years to recognize and accept the fact that whenever his wife had a cold she lost her sense of taste, and when she was depressed she lost her appetite!

NTs can carry their drive for competence into the home. They make it another proving ground for themselves. They may carry their risk-taking into the home, too, and jeopardize the family's future as they do so. They devote much of their interest on new things that can be done in the home. One wife and mother will probably never finish any of the homes she has bought or had built. As fast as she changes one part of the house, she sees something else to do somewhere else.

NTs can vary significantly as parents. Many NTs, male or female, see their parenting role as yet another area for them to demonstrate their competence. These NTs may add to their love of their children an endless and consistent attention to being effective parents. Those who do not see parenting in that light may be loving parents but are likely to be inconsistent ones, devoting energy and attention to their children some of the time and being disinterested or uninvolved at others.

A Final Word

NTs have a sense of the big picture. They are intellectually curious and analytical. They think bold new thoughts and want to bring about better worlds. They are willing to take risks and skate on thin ice in the service of a good cause. These attributes make them powerful and interesting people, particularly when they can avoid their temperament's pitfalls—elitism, arrogance, impatience with details, disregard for constituted authority, and a lack of sensitivity to others' feelings.

ENTJ

ENTJs look at the world around them and see judgments—impersonal, analytical judgments—that need to be made. They see people and things to be organized. They see new and innovative challenges all around them. And they want to be the ones to make it all happen. They want to do the leading.

Of all the types, only the ESTJ feels a similar leadership drive. ENTJs and ESTJs share a desire to be in positions of influence and control. Where the two types differ is in the kinds of leadership positions they seek and what gifts they bring to those positions. ENTJs often look for positions that offer them opportunities to strike off in new directions, to satisfy their entrepreneurial and creative instincts.

ENTJs move surely and confidently into the external world. They see things and people that need organizing. They don't start out with a preconceived blueprint for what they want to do. They see the need as it presents itself to them. They are "take-charge" people.

Even young ENTJs demonstrate an instinctive drive for leadership. A 15-year-old ENTJ asked his mother to drive him to where his friends were building their homecoming float. He just wanted to see what was going on. He came back in charge. His class won first prize. For the next two years, he was in charge, and all three years his class won first prize.

As a senior, his interests had matured. He overheard his teachers complaining that their county ranked second or third in the nation in per capita income. They also ranked 127th in teachers' salaries. That made the young man angry. Within two weeks he had organized "Students for Teachers" in his county. He put students to work collecting petitions. He organized students and parents to speak to the School Board and the Board of Supervisors. And he loved every minute of it.

ENTJs' interest in new or entrepreneurial ventures comes from their preference for focusing on possibilities. They are quick to grasp complexities, and they enjoy making connections and seeing relationships. As leaders, therefore, they focus on the large picture. They see things in long range terms. They want to provide overall direction and leave the detailed execution to subordinates. They are, therefore, change oriented leaders. They will reshape an organization's goals and seek more efficient ways of getting the job done.

Even as parents, they reflect their "I'm in charge here" personalities. One young ISFP noticed a pattern in how his father came home from work. He invariably went straight to either the TV or the stereo to turn it down or off. "I think Dad does that," observed the young man, "just to show he's the boss."

At an early age, ENTJs begin to manifest their drive for closure. When they are young and dependent on others for transportation, for example, they want things settled—on the spot. It is unfair to see that behavior as a manifestation of a childish need for "instant gratification." Before making that judgment, watch their reaction to being told they cannot have what they want. Do they become angry but quickly get over it? The chances are that they have reflected on the decision, accepted it as final, and made other plans. They are now ready to move on. It is often useful, then, to ignore initial angry reactions. Confronting anger with anger is likely to block ENTJs' ability to re-decide and to prolong their outburst.

Do not, however, look for young ENTJs to be organized and orderly, to keep their rooms neat, or to make lists. Their need for having things settled does not extend to such matters as these!

The speed with which ENTJs make judgments and the confidence they have in themselves often make them somewhat overpowering personalities. They can, in short, be intimidating people. Many ENTJs expect others to show similar strengths and are sharply critical of those who do not. It is, in short, often difficult for ENTJs to listen to those who do not "speak their language." Thus, in leadership positions, they can deprive themselves of important information from subordinates who fear to speak up. ENTJs are more likely than most types to surround themselves with other ENTJs, thus reinforcing their strengths but at the same time compounding their weaknesses.

Some ENTJs are so decision-oriented, so quick to form judgments, that they run the risk of making hasty judgments or of forming judgments based on insufficient information. Other ENTJs appreciate the need for decisions based on good data. These ENTJs have a strong reflective side that brings balance to their personalities. They enjoy time alone, for that is when they feel the need to reflect. The need for making decisions recedes. They turn things over in their minds. They look at things from different perspectives. They find new insights and discover new possibilities.

Even reflective ENTJs, however, want to have things settled. They, too, make quick decisions and act confidently on them. They will, though, remain open to reconsidering decisions when challenged or given new information. They arrange their lives or their schedules so that they can have time to reflect.

Put several ENTJs side-by-side and they seem very different. Some are "hard." They appear really cold and impersonal, giving orders and brooking no opposition. Others seem "warm" or "soft." They are more aware of people and more collaborative in their decision-making process. And it's not a male-female difference. The difference lies in the extent to which they give themselves time for inner reflection. Balanced and truly powerful ENTJs have a private side, a need to turn inward periodically to explore intuitive possibilities.

While ENTJs can focus on details, they are more likely to do so when in the service of an intuitive insight or in support of a thinking judgment. Facts alone do not interest them very much. Indeed, they are likely to get impatient if they have to deal with details for very long. Details are for others, not for them, for the next bold stroke or large issue is always there to beckon them away.

Judgments based on personal values constitute ENTJs' least developed side. They are often unaware of the impact of their behavior on others, and they are often unaware of how others are feeling. ENTJs are least skilled at deciding things on the basis of personal values. They are uncomfortable with decisions that involve being sensitive to people and their emotions.

When under stress or down on themselves, however, ENTJs will often make value-laden, subjective judgments about themselves or others. If they express these judgments, they may do so with an explosive outburst. ENTJs can have terrible tempers! They can use feeling judgments as a weapon to beat up on themselves. They can use them to challenge their accomplishments, their competence, or their self-esteem.

On the other hand, ENTJs are also likely to have a strong sentimental streak. Inside, they can have emotional attachments to people, groups, or ideals that defy logical explanation. Some ENTJs may see the sentimental side of themselves as a sign of weakness. They often seek to mask it with gruffness, thinking no one will notice! Sometimes, their value-based or people-centered judgments are ill-conceived —childish, even— and, if acted upon can cause them trouble.

The ENTJ personality is a strong one. Unlike many of the other psychological types, ENTJs do not need to assert themselves or get out of their own way in order to live up to their potential. For them the challenge is to avoid the tendency to make hasty decisions, to act on them before checking them out, to fail to encourage others to speak up, to dismiss opposing points of view without consideration, to forget that a sensitivity to people is an important part of life. Those ENTJs who develop the discipline to avoid these pitfalls are truly powerful people in the best sense of that word.

INTJ

INTJs orient their lives around turning inner visions into reality. What those inner visions are vary from one INTJ to another. With some, it may be a sense of what their organizations might become. With others, it may be a conviction about a new architectural form. With still others, it may be a warning that society needs to hear. Or it may be a commitment to a different use of the media.

What INTJs have in common is an inner driving force that generates possibilities. They have a special kind of intuitive power deep within them. They keep this most important part of themselves to themselves. Inside, when alone, they see all kinds of far-reaching and usually impersonal insights. They turn these insights over and over from many different angles, building possibilities on possibilities. Their insights are most often centered on ideas, not people—on principles, not values.

INTJs are very much at home in the world of abstractions, of theories, of patterns of thought. They see bold new designs, new ways of doing things, new futures to shape. From deep down inside them, INTJs see unusual and powerful possibilities, sometimes of a sweeping nature. They have great confidence in these insights of theirs, and they find in them their most important life direction.

Sometimes what they see inside is not totally clear to them. Clearly delineated or not, they know that they should act on them. And so they do, often paying little or no attention to discouraging remarks from others. They often ignore warning signs that what they want to do won't work. INTJs can be very stubborn personalities indeed!

INTJs have faith in their insights and ideas. They trust the plans and judgments they make about what to do with them. They are decisive, self-confident personalities—sometimes intellectually arrogant ones. INTJs are often unaware that this is the impression they give. They are so intent on turning their inner visions into realities that they don't recognize how their behavior affects others.

They seem sometimes to listen with half an ear to the conversation taking place around them. Their real attention is focused on their inner intuitive responses. They may anticipate what others will say and interrupt them with their own reactions. Or they may cut off a conversation with peers or subordinates, because their important inner guidance system has provided the information or insight they need.

A major challenge for some INTJs is not to place too much faith in their own inner insights. INTJs who do so become extremely rigid personalities. What seems to happen is this: They get some information. They have an instant and powerful inner reaction. They just know that their inner reaction is correct. And they let others know it! They come across to others as believing there is such a thing as Absolute Truth. They act as if they know what it is with regard to almost any subject. Provide these INTJs with some data, and they are likely to respond with great vehemence: "Nonsense" and then proceed to say what the truth of the matter is. Having any kind of meaningful conversation with these INTJs is not possible.

One such INTJ participated in a management training program. With the other participants, he watched a video-taped interview. The participants were to make notes on the statements and behaviors of the person being interviewed. During the discussion after the tape, the INTJ suddenly interjected: "Well, I'd never hire that man. He's . . . " and he proceeded to give his judgment about the person.

The trainer, in an attempt to be polite, ignored the fact that the INTJ had not done he was asked to do. He replied: "Oh, what's your evidence?"

The INTJ instantly described what he believed the person to have said or done. The trainer, trying to be polite but firm, said: "I wish we had time to replay the tape, but we don't. Let me just say that I have probably watched this tape 400 times, and he made none of the statements you have ascribed to him."

To which the INTJ simply folded his hands across his chest, shook his head and muttered, "I still wouldn't hire the guy."

INTJs approach everything from an intellectually skeptical point of view. That can be either a strength or a weakness. The INTJs' natural style works well when a theoretical discussion leads to understanding and clarity. Their intellectual skepticism gets in the way, however, when learning is best achieved by suspending judgment, by experiencing something and then judging on the basis of the experience. INTJs can be very resistant to trying any style of learning other than their own.

Control is a very important issue in the lives of some INTJs. For them, the goal is that they are in conscious control of their behavior—all of it. They believe that doing things spontaneously leads to trouble or is a sign of weakness. They may believe that having one's emotions or psychological needs control them means being out of control. "I don't believe," said one INTJ, "that anyone should ever act on an emotional decision. I've seen too many battlefield commanders make bad mistakes that way."

Outwardly, INTJs are impersonal, analytical, crisp, and disciplined. They are quick to share their judgments with others. They are often commanding personalities who like leadership roles and successfully seek them. They can be excellent leaders or managers, particularly in situations that call for a reexamination of the mission of the organization, for a new sense of purpose or direction. In leadership roles, they often need to push themselves to be clear about what they are thinking. That's not easy because of their tendency to keep their inner intuitive insights to themselves. It's even more difficult when those insights are somewhat unclear even to them. INTJs have faith in them—but how can others act on what they don't know or understand or have no experience of?

INTJs are not particularly sensitive to people and values. They themselves avoid making subjective and value based decisions. So caught up are they in deciding things impersonally and analytically that they may not see when situations call for a more people-oriented way of deciding things. When INTJs do recognize the need to focus their decision-making on people and values, they achieve a balanced perspective that can contribute to success in whatever they undertake to do.

INTJs' least developed side has to do with facts and realities, the details of life. They can get quickly frustrated when they must deal with details, particularly when the details are not related to one of their intuitive insights. Facts alone have very little meaning for them.

INTJs have a tendency to go to extremes with regard to details. They can become obsessed with details. They collect them endlessly to no purpose. They make no useful distinctions between ones that are important and ones that are not. They think that their grasp of the details is absolutely correct. Or, at the other extreme, they simply ignore details. They remain oblivious to the most obvious, immediate and important factual information. They can become furious with colleagues or subordinates if challenged on their handling of details. They see themselves as having a firm and accurate grasp on what is needed and what is important.

When caught up in the grip of a low self image, however, when under stress or down on themselves, INTJs can get obsessed with details in a self-destructive way. When at their most self critical, they often use facts to demonstrate to themselves that they are incompetent. The world of details becomes a weapon turned on themselves.

INTJs are powerful personalities. They are often intellectually creative and academically gifted. They have an unusual ability to set challenging goals for themselves and promptly and successfully set out to achieve them—in whatever field or activity they select. One study of marathoners, for example, found that of all the sixteen types, INTJs were most likely to decide to run that 26 mile distance in under three hours and do it—the first time!

ENTP

ENTPs focus their attention on the world around them and see endless and fascinating possibilities. They react with high energy and enthusiasm and are particularly effective at persuading others to join in their adventures. Their lives do not often conform to a single pattern. Instead, they follow their intuitive insights wherever they lead. They may move from one field of study to another, from one career to another, from one interest to another.

An ENTP college student, for example, thoroughly enjoyed his first two years at a liberal arts college. Undergraduates there had the freedom to take whatever courses they pleased. They were not restricted to a prescribed distribution of courses. Typically, he took advantage of a college policy that allowed him a few weeks to decide on his course schedule. He enrolled in those courses he thought interesting. He attended all of them, and when he was sure of his choices, dropped those he was less interested in.

He dreaded having to declare a major. In part to avoid having to do so, he spent his junior year in a special work program. He did not want to limit his options! Another ENTP student, struggling academically though very bright, responded to someone who asked what he was going to do the next academic year by saying: "I don't know. I'm in a 'comma' in my life right now."

Before he turned 40, a very talented ENTP computer programming expert started several businesses and then left them. He consistently found himself so successful at obtaining business that he had to hire others to help. Soon he was managing a small business. He'd get tired of it and either disband or sell the business. Within a short period of time he'd repeat the process all over again. And through it all, he explored other lines of work or study that he thought might excite him more.

ENTPs are one of two types (ENFP being the other) whom people frequently ask: "What are you going to do when you grow up?" They will hear that question long after they have become mature and effective adults. Why? Because others see them as being fickle. They do not settle down in a career or profession and commit their lives to the pursuit of it. What others don't see, however, is that ENTPs are not fickle at all. They are constant and faithful to one overriding source of energy—their inspirations. They go where their energy takes them. They move after whatever strikes them as the most powerful possibility. Some ENTPs do stay within a single career path. Why? Because they find it rich enough or varied enough to allow full play for their intuitive gifts.

Effective ENTPs examine their inspirations and intuitive insights logically and analytically. Their world is too full of exciting possibilities. They understand the need to decide which ones are truly worth devoting themselves to. ENTPs who have a well developed reflective side are often powerful and penetrating personalities. In Myers' phrase, they can have "insights amounting to wisdom"

ENTPs who do not exercise their logical and analytical abilities can pay a particularly heavy price for failing to do so. They run the risk of moving from one possibility to another, without ever completing anything. They leave a trail of unfinished business, unfulfilled opportunities, behind them.

Without the balance that logical and impersonal judgments provide them, they can be impulsive, undependable, irresponsible. They follow whatever whim happens to hit them at any given moment. They are truly "fickle" personalities. They frustrate and disappoint all those who know and care for them.

The combination of possibilities and logic makes ENTPs more interested in philosophical considerations than people. They pay less attention to personal values than to principles, laws and dynamics of things. Intellectual things interest them. They often have a fascination for the life of the mind. They enjoy arguing for the sake of arguing. They often have a need to be intellectually one-up. They can pursue one-upsmanship at times without regard for whether that behavior is hurtful, boring, or frustrating to others. Life can be an intellectual game to them, one they are very good at and enjoy playing. And they play it very competitively.

ENTPs are not inclined to be impressed with authority unless it is the authority of competence. They may not, however, confront authority head-on. They are more likely to make a game of out-witting it. They maneuver around it. They set up those in authority to embarrass or poke fun at. In fact, much of life is a charming, happy game for ENTPs. They have a way of pulling rabbits out of hats, going with the flow, finding a pot at the end of a rainbow.

ENTPs' combination of preferences makes them flexible, ingenious at finding different ways of doing things, and charmingly irreverent. They are full of ideas, energy and enthusiasm. They often juggle many things at once. They get by with brilliance, with a flair for the dramatic—and by the skin of their teeth.

Often their best inspirations do not come to them until what others would consider the last minute (and beyond). Only then do the bursts of insight and energy come. Some ENTPs think that their work style is a weakness and criticize themselves for working that way. Were they to try to do their work in a methodical, scheduled fashion, however, it is likely that projects would not only take much longer but be dull as dishwater as well! Their particular challenge is not to handle so much or put things off so long that they cannot complete an assignment or project at all. It is a delicate and sometimes difficult line for many ENTPs to draw for themselves. Those who do are often very successful.

With effort, ENTPs can see the people-and-value side of things. They sometimes make and share judgments that show an awareness of emotional content. They can, if they set their minds to it, take into account their own values and the values of others. Being aware of people-and-value con-siderations does not come naturally to them. They may, for example, play their one- upsmanship games long after it is apparent to others that they are unnecessarily upsetting or hurting others.

ENTPs are least skilled at handling details. In the pursuit of their intuitive insights, ENTPs often do not want to know about the details. When details become clearly important, they will deal with them. And not before. When ENTPs must deal with the details of daily living—for example, balan-cing a checkbook— they are likely to feel depressed, bored, or frustrated. They avoid dealing with them as long as possible. One ENTP has never balanced her checkbook. When she "senses" she may be close to overdrawing her account, she stops writing checks for ten days. At that time, she calls the bank, asks what her balance is, accepts it as accurate, and begins to write more checks. She figures that if her creditors have not cashed her checks in ten days, that's their problem!

At another extreme, ENTPs can become fascinated with details. They will set out to prove to themselves that they can handle the details of daily living precisely and accurately. What is hap-pening? These ENTPs find an intellectual challenge relating to details. One ENTP, for example, en-joyed setting up systems to handle the details of his financial life. Then the details would take care of themselves. What these ENTPs don't see is how unusual this kind of behavior is with them. They don't see how often they are blissfully unaware of important details.

When down on themselves, however, ENTPs often search for factual evidence to prove that their lives have any meaning. They find it very difficult to focus on anything but the most pessimistic of data. They may not be aware of, or attend to, their physical needs. They can seem oblivious to the need for rest. It may make take serious health problems to slow them down. An ENTP woman in her 70's has more than once gone on vacations to Europe or the Caribbean shortly after serious knee operations that demanded more recuperative time than she was willing to give. And she wonders why she suffers so much pain from arthritis!

Altogether, only ENFPs challenge ENTPs in the range of their interests and abilities. They have, to use Isabel Myers' phrase, many possible "paths to excellence" available to them. Like other types, to use Myers' words again, they have their "pitfalls to be avoided." It is important, for example, for ENTPs is build "alone time" into their lives. For that is when they begin to look critically at the many possibilities they see in the world around them. That is when they sort out the wheat from the chaff. When alone, they make their best judgments about what they want to do next. Time alone brings balance to ENTPs, and balanced ENTPs are powerful, charming and often gifted personalities.

INTP

The most important characteristic of INTPs is a drive for conceptual clarity. When alone, their minds naturally turn to drawing conclusions or making judgments on patterns of thought. Unusually skilled at impersonal analysis, they are drawn to conceptual riddles as iron filings are drawn to magnets. Unfortunately, as soon as they solve one, they find another— often before they have followed through to the point where others can benefit from their work.

INTPs often think in terms of classification schemes. They seek to find patterns in anything that interests them. When they discover one, they want to identify the logical explanation for it. Thus, patterns and logical explanations often constitute an obsession for INTPs.

INTPs find important fulfillment in developing useful conceptual schemes. That is when they credit themselves for making contributions to their field of specialty. But INTPs can get carried away with conceptualizing. Some try to treat all life as one great conceptual puzzle. They want to reduce everything to a set of classification schemes and corresponding intellectual explanations. Friends and associates can find that behavior extremely frustrating.

Internally, INTPs want order. They want things figured out. Sometimes their internal need for order manifests itself externally. They want to have their own physical space—their offices or their automobiles, for example—to be clean, organized and orderly. It's almost as if by cleaning up their external world they find that they can concentrate better on their internal puzzles. Sometimes, though, cleaning up their work space is their way of avoiding the hard work of thinking through and writing about all those classification schemes!

And INTPs are not consistently organized in their external worlds, either, no matter how much they say they want to be, no matter how much they try. They go through predictable cycles. Things get impossibly disorganized. They spend hours cleaning everything up. Soon everything is a mess again!

Nor are they any better at managing their time or their appointments. The very skill they have at organizing inner patterns of thought seems totally lacking when it comes to keeping their external worlds organized. They can make three appointments for the same lunch and not be aware of it until the disaster is upon them. They can write down obligations and then lose the piece of paper they've written them on or forget to look at it until too late. Many of the stories of "absent-minded professors" have to have been written about INTPs.

More often than not, INTPs are easy-going personalities. They move effortlessly—and sometimes enthusiastically—from one intuitive insight to another. Some INTPs, however, are consistently formal and somewhat distant with all but their closest friends.

Too much time in extraverted activities can cause INTPs to become disorganized and to have extreme difficulty following things through to completion. On the other hand, too much time alone can cause them to make hasty, theoretical judgments based on insufficient data. Still, INTPs need time alone to do their best work. Some have difficulty protecting their introverted time, because they want to be responsive to others. In short, they may find it difficult to say "no" particularly if exciting possibilities are involved.

In meetings, INTPs may become silent and withdrawn. When that happens, they are usually trying to figure things out. They want to achieve that all-important internal clarity before contributing. When—or if—they do speak up, they often present a "blueprint," a complete and detailed conceptual statement of the issue at hand.

They can listen to a formal presentation, turn over in their minds long, complex arguments, and then prepare a written or oral summary that captures the central thesis and its supporting arguments—together with an analysis of its strengths and weaknesses. Asked prematurely for their conclusions, summaries or analyses, however, and they will either seem awkward or unprepared or will try to "buy time" by distracting the questioner.

INTPs can have problems communicating their ideas effectively. They deal easily with conceptual complexities. They want to share with others the conceptual subtleties they see as so important. They end up overwhelming others. In short, they can lose, confuse, or bore others. INTPs who want to make a difference need to work constantly on developing their communications skills. They need to work hard to simplify what they say or write. They need to work even harder to develop a sensitivity to their audience's level of toleration for what they are saying.

INTPs can be impatient, bored or frustrated when dealing with facts and realities. They need to give themselves time alone when dealing with the details of daily living. They need to avoid punishing themselves for making mistakes. With patience and time alone, they begin to see progress. Eventually they derive a sense of pleasure and satisfaction in their successful handling of what to them are boring details.

With details related to intuitive possibilities or to the solution of conceptual problems, it is another matter. INTPs can be patient and painstaking when working with specifics necessary to support an insight or round out a theory. If the project is important enough, they can become perfectionists. They have trouble knowing when a piece of work is "good enough."

Socially, INTPs are often extremely shy. They have trouble meeting people, particularly in casual settings. Making "cocktail party" conversation is very difficult for them. They feel awkward and find themselves tongue-tied. It is quite different when they are with people they know well or are discussing a familiar and important subject. Many INTPs become so outgoing and confident that others have trouble believing that they are, in fact, introverts. And when INTPs meet someone for whom they feel a powerful attraction, they often find the resources to overcome their social reserve.

INTPs can form close attachments and be steadfast and loyal friends. If, however, they believe that they have been betrayed, they may change overnight and become cold, distant, and aloof. If they believe a friend has violated one of their most cherished principles, they may abruptly terminate a relationship. The change can be startling, hurtful and puzzling to those to whom it happens, particularly if they do not know what they have done.

Once the bond is broken, INTPs are not likely to rebuild a relationship. They were once free, spontaneous, and open. Now, even if they talk about what has happened, they find that they are monitoring carefully everything they say or do. The difference between the former spontaneity and the present guardedness is too unpleasant. The relationship, no matter how enriching and exciting it once was, no longer seems worth continuing.

INTPs are not often aware of others' feelings or how their behavior affects others. They concentrate almost totally on the content of any conversation. They simply do not absorb at a conscious level the important people considerations. As instructors, they may go straight through break time. They may be ignorant of the fact that they have exceeded participants' attention spans.

Nor are INTPs adept at making value judgments. To them, judgments based on personal values—their own or others—are one step removed from personal prejudice. They violate the objectivity, the logic, that they strive so hard to achieve.

Under stress or the influence of drugs and alcohol or when suffering from low self esteem, INTPs fall into making subjective value judgments. Under pressure, they may express angry judgments about almost anything that gets in their way. When discouraged, they make negative value judgments about themselves. They judge themselves as incompetent. Once stuck in these negative judgments, INTPs can find it very difficult to get unstuck. One INTP, whose father and father-in-law were very good with tools, dreaded doing anything having to do with tools. He was sure he would botch anything he worked on. He saw in his failures evidence that he was not a competent male!

INTPs live so completely in the conceptual world that they may lack meaningful personal relationships. Too long deprived, the need for relationships can surface in a sudden and overwhelming attraction. They can find themselves swept off their feet by their own emotional intensity. INTPs can fall in love with love, idealizing out of all proportion the object of their affections.

INTPs are outstanding conceptualizers. They are usually clear-headed thinkers. They can deal effectively with complex abstractions. They are often powerful theoreticians. "Scratch an INTP," says David Keirsey, himself an INTP, "and you'll find Machiavelli."

They are not as adept in human relationships. They often find it difficult to initiate conversations. INTPs can use all the help and understanding they can get from other types to break through their shyness. Those who do will often discover, along with their intellectual gifts, energy, excitement and warmth.

V The NF Temperament

All those who share preferences for intuition and feeling (ENFJ, INFJ, ENFP, and INFP) constitute one of Keirsey's four temperaments. They view the world in terms of possibilities, relationships, connections and meanings— particularly with regard to people. They make decisions based on values. They identify and act on what matters to them and to others. Their decisions focus on people concerns.

Keirsey, in fact, calls NFs Catalysts. They see possibilities in people. They want to contribute to human potential. They want to bring out the best in themselves and others. They want life to have a personal meaning for themselves. They want to help others find meaning and fulfillment in what they are and do.

"How are you going to distribute the brochure once it is written?" asked an NF of an NT. The question came as a surprise to the NT. He and a group of NFs were discussing how to organize the results of more than twenty interviews.

"I don't know," responded the NT. His energies were directed at making some logical order out of a mass of material. "Find out when the people for whom the brochure is being written come on board. Then send it to them with a memo from the Director of Personnel."

"Wouldn't the brochure have greater impact on the new people we are trying to help if we involved some experienced staffers? We could ask if they think it's a good brochure. If they do, we could suggest they introduce themselves to newcomers and offer to help. They could give them a copy of the brochure and tell them that they think it's a good introduction to their new role."

The NT was stunned. He knew the idea would never have occurred to him. "That's a great idea," he said, "let's do it." And he promptly dropped the subject. For him, the central challenge was to identify how to organize in crisp and logical fashion all the information in twenty interviews. He would leave the people-oriented part of the strategy to the NF.

NFs, then, are the people possibility people. That is their happiest, their life-long focus. Some are exuberant personalities. They respond to and get their direction from their contacts with people. Some are more quiet and introspective. They get a surer sense of purpose from inner reflection. Some are organized, directed and disciplined. Some are spontaneous and impulsive, moving and changing as the flow of life suggests.

NFs are empathic personalities. They have a well developed awareness of self and others. They are sensitive to their own emotions and those of others. Some show their warmth. They are, as Isabel Myers suggested, like fur coats. The warmth is immediately apparent. Others are like a fur-lined coat. The warmth shows only when they choose.

When NFs express appreciation, it is almost always directed personally, not at what others have said or done. "You know," an NF might say to an NT, "I really enjoy working with you. You are an exciting person to work with." Other temperaments are more likely to say: "That was a great job you did. You really cut through to the essential points."

The NF style can embarrass other temperaments, and they may not know how to respond. An NT responded to personal praise from an NF by saying: "Rob, I have a difficult consulting situation coming up. I'd really like to pick your brains about it."

The NF was hurt. He heard no acknowledgement, only a change in the subject. He said as much to the NT, who looked puzzled and said: "Don't you understand? My asking you to help me think through this situation is giving you the highest praise I can think of!"

Basic to the NF temperament is a life-long search for identity. With other temperaments, there may be the identity crisis of adolescence and, perhaps, another at mid-life. With NFs, the "who am I?" question is an on-going one. As soon as they arrive at one answer, they raise the question again. There is always a deeper level of meaning to discover.

For some, the question and the search is a happy and productive one. For others, the search may be productive, but also difficult. For a few, however, the search is both difficult and paralytic. These NFs struggle with the issue. They somehow cannot get from life or from within themselves the resources to find the answers or to live up to their ideals.

The NF search for meaning is often not limited to self. Many NFs have natural skills at seeing and drawing out the human potential of others. NTs see potential in others, too, but it's a different kind. NTs see in others a potential competence. They recognize what others can achieve if they develop their competence. Some NTs dedicate their lives to helping others see their own competence and live up to it.

NFs, on the other hand, do not analyze people in terms of competence or potential competence. They see people as human beings, who, as Shakespeare had Richard II say of himself and of kings,

> For you have but mistook me all this while:
> I live with bread like you, feel want,
> Taste grief, need friends—subjected thus,
> How can you say to me, I am a King?

Looking at people the way they do, many NFs want to dedicate themselves to helping others to experience their human-ness. They want to help others to understand themselves as human beings, to realize their potential as individuals. They want to help others find their own identity and to live up to their own human potential. They want to help others with the pains and sorrows, the joys and laughter of life. Is it any wonder, then, that many NFs seek careers in the helping professions?

NFs are especially aware of and sensitive to the interpersonal atmosphere. They can assess quickly the emotional environment of a situation. They bring harmony to any relationship, group or organization they are part of. And they need for themselves what they so naturally give to others—harmony. They suffer more than other temperaments in conflict situations—only ESFJs and ISFJs come close. And they will often give way or sacrifice their own needs for the sake of harmony.

It would be easy to conclude that NFs are emotional patsies. In fact, some of them are. The judgment, however, is overdrawn. Most NFs have a line, a point past which they cannot or will not be pushed. When that point is reached, NFs are, perhaps, more effectively dispassionate than any of the other temperaments. They can be extraordinarily effective in confronting individuals or groups with how their behavior affects relationships or group productivity.

NFs, in short, can be particularly effective in situations that call for conflict resolution. When a conflict includes them, they can still play a powerful peace-making role, but often at the expense of inner turmoil. Even when they are not personally involved, some NFs have problems remaining detached. Others learn to remain sensitive to conflict situations but personally detached. They are the fortunate ones, for they are effective in conflict resolution roles without themselves being drained emotionally.

A weakness that can afflict NFs is self-centeredness. Sometimes NFs are caught up in their own search for identity to the exclusion of anything or anyone else. Sometimes their own personal need for harmony overshadows all other considerations. Then the world truly and powerfully revolves around self. Some NFs are this way when young, others never quite outgrow it.

In some NFs, the self-centeredness is clear, overt and direct. Others mask it. They may seek self-affirmation, for example, through a friendliness toward others that is overdone, too eager, too quick to seek intimacy. Or they may involve themselves in helping activities or relationships when others have not asked for and may not desire help.

NFs can also suffer acutely from a special brand of guilt. They can do a "guilt trip" on themselves when they do not live up to the standards they set for themselves. Or they can hold themselves responsible when their efforts to help others "fail"—that is, when others do not, choose not, or cannot respond to their efforts to help. And many NFs are particularly vulnerable when others criticize them for "failure"—failure to live up to others' expectations or failure to have been successful in helping others. There may be nothing quite so guilty as the guilt NFs can feel! Some may even make a profession of it. They wallow in self- reproach. They paralyze themselves from accomplishing anything or do not give themselves credit for what they do accomplish.

As is so often the case, what we do to ourselves, we do to others. And so it is that NFs are without a doubt the most creative of all temperaments in inducing guilt in others. When others do not do what NFs want, NFs may say whatever they think will make others feel guilty. Sometimes, NFs don't even use words—they can just look at another person and transmit the message. Sometimes NFs make appropriate use their ability to make others feel guilty. Sometimes NFs use their ability inappropriately. When coupled with self-centeredness, their guilt-inducing behavior can be destructive to themselves, to others and to their relationships.

NFs are also the most seductive of the temperaments. They can talk their way into or out of almost anything. They can do the most outrageous things and get away with them. NFs can behave in such a way that it's almost impossible to stay angry with them. It is often difficult to express anger or disapproval at what they do.

When others criticize them, NFs have a tendency to personalize the criticism. They often have difficulty separating themselves from what they do. Many NFs, therefore, build elaborate defense strategies for deflecting criticism. A favorite strategy is what might be called the moving target. That is, they constantly shift the focus of the discussion so that those with whom they are dealing cannot pursue the point they want to get across!

NF seductivity includes themselves, for effective seduction, after all, begins at home. NFs can be powerfully creative at rationalizing anything they do, and the first person persuaded is often themselves. Thus, NFs can get stuck, particularly emotionally, but also with regard to their behavior or positions they take. They can paralyze themselves from doing anything to change. They can be extremely resistant, however engagingly, to any efforts on the part of others to help them get unstuck!

Relationships with NFs are sometimes frustratingly difficult.

NFs and the World of Work

Like the rest of us, NFs gravitate toward work that will give them opportunities to express their natural gifts. They seek out organizations whose mission involves human potential. They want to work with people. They want to help others to live fulfilling and meaningful lives. Many find careers in the helping professions, like counselling or therapy. Others are attracted to religious professions. Many enjoy teaching.

NFs find organizations whose mission does not directly involve human potential both dehumanizing and limiting. They avoid them if at all possible. Those who do work in such organizations often seek human resource development or other specialized roles that allow them to satisfy their people-possibility needs. Otherwise, NFs are usually either unhappy or feel distinctly out of place. They almost always yearn to be someplace else, to do something different.

An NF motorcycle salesman dislikes having to "cut the best deal possible" with every sale. He dreams of a job where he can sell energy-conservation devices and thereby help both individuals and mankind. In the meantime, he asks his boss to give him a different role. He would prefer to concentrate on selling parts and accessories where prices are set and there is no haggling. There, at least, he can relate to people, learn what they want and show them the possibilities.

Another NF, whose career path led to auditing, excels at helping those whom he audits feel comfortable with him. He devotes his energy to the "service" as opposed to the "police" aspects of his role. Yet he continues to feel out of place and unfulfilled. He talks of going back to school to become a therapist. Then he learns of a field of consulting—Organization Development—where the consultant helps people in organizations work more effectively together. He thinks perhaps that he can move into that field. He can combine experience as an auditor with his interest in helping people.

Not many NFs become managers except in those organizations that directly deal with human potential, such as career counselling centers, mental health organizations, churches, or non-profit institutions. The work of a manager appeals more to TJs, for managing is often seen as involving logical, analytical, impersonal decisions (T), the purpose of which is to bring order and productivity to the external world (J).

There are, of course, NF managers. Many perform excellently. They bring their special gifts to their work as managers. When NF managers are put in groups to discuss their strengths and weaknesses as managers (without being told that they are NFs!), they report out that they believe that they are good at things like:

- bringing out the best in people
- helping people to work effectively together
- creating and maintaining morale
- building a harmonious working environment
- listening

They cite things they don't do well or don't like to do:

- disciplining employees for poor performance
- working in an atmosphere of hostility or distrust
- handling details
- dealing well with criticism

In short, the lists of qualities NFs bring to the world of work have a marked people-possibility focus. In addition, they are often sensitive to the core values of the organization. They are concerned that the organization live up to these values and make the best use of its human resources. There is some evidence to suggest that Thomas Jefferson and Abraham Lincoln were NFs.

Some NF managers concentrate too much on the human equation and end up putting people before task. A happy organization does not always mean a productive one. Sometimes NFs think the two are the same. Unfortunately, even when NF managers effectively balance people and tasks, their TJ colleagues may not credit them for it. TJ managers see NFs as "soft" when they may not be at all. Why? Because many TJ managers have never considered that managing means getting things done through others!

One management consultant, apparently not knowing anything about Keirsey's temperaments, describes four basic types of managers. He has two terms for each group. For one of them, he uses the terms Integrator and Super-follower. Integrators sound like effective NF managers. They mobilize the human resources of the organization to get the work done. Super-followers also sound like NFs. They attach themselves to the boss, giving him or her unquestioned loyalty, blindly following where the other leads.

NF Children and Students

NF children and students are often creative and charming. As with adults, NF students have a wide range of interests and abilities. They are generally gifted either in verbal or written skills or both. They often have artistic or musical interests or gifts. They enjoy subjects that call on their love of fantasy, that involve their active imaginations. NFs are not turned on by subjects that involve painstaking attention to detail. Routine is not one of their strong suits. They grasp abstractions effortlessly and see interconnections astonishingly quickly.

NF students are more likely than others to be responsive to teachers of all temperaments—if they create a supportive environment. In fact, NFs flourish best in warm and supportive atmospheres—in the home or at school. Tensions at home or a teacher perceived as cold, distant and critical can have a powerful negative effect on NFs. When NF students like a teacher, they will work doubly hard. NF children and young people like to please, and they respond well to praise.

Criticism is quite another matter. NFs' sensitivity to criticism begins at an early age. Their tendency to take criticism personally makes them particularly vulnerable when young. Criticism, coupled with a tense or hostile environment, can be particularly devastating to NF young people. They are likely to suffer a loss of confidence and self-esteem and become paralyzed emotionally and intellectually.

The need to please, the desire for harmony, the sensitivity to criticism are life-long attributes of NFs. Some of them will go to such lengths to please and to maintain harmony that they will ignore their own emotional needs. In the end, these NFs pay a price—either in emotional distress or physical illness, or both.

In NF children, seductiveness starts early. It is not uncommon for NF youngsters to get into trouble and charm their way out of it. As with NF adults, others often find it difficult to stay angry with young NFs who have clearly done something they should not have done. Sometimes NF children can get willful and stubborn, dig in their heels and resist efforts to redirect their energies. At an early age NFs begin to develop the "moving target" defense when called on the carpet!

NFs and Adult Relationships

NFs contribute a lot to relationships. They are full of empathy, caring, warmth and harmony. They have a sense of curiosity and wonder about people and the world around and beyond. Some bring energy and enthusiasm—charisma, even—to relationships. Others are more gentle, are quieter and more soft spoken. However they manifest their NF qualities, their behaviors help create harmonious and supportive environments for friends and family. The search for identity and meaning, for self and others, is an exciting one, and few can chart that course better than NFs.

Romance is an important part of the life of NFs. They can create a dreamy ideal of what love or a life's partner should look like and spend their lives looking for that particular "Holy Grail." Today's partner somehow never seems quite good enough. There must be someone more perfect out there somewhere. Carried too far, these NFs second-guess every important relationship they have. They plague themselves with guilt or self doubt, or both.

Other NFs go to the opposite extreme. When committed to a relationship, they idealize their partners. They see them through life-long rose-colored lenses. They remember and celebrate a romance that never ends. The phrase, "falling in love with love," aptly describes many of these NFs.

Still other NFs fall in love with the dating game—the chase. They can pursue with great energy and imagination someone who strikes their fancy—until that person says "yes." At that point, some of the fun is gone and their interest turns elsewhere. Some of these NFs become what can only be called "sexual athletes" or teases. They may— though many would deny it—hurt those who see a commitment that is not there.

When are NFs not fun to be around? When self-centeredness takes over. When they get down on themselves and wallow in "oh, woe is me" despair. When they are doing a guilt trip on themselves or are actively dishing out guilt trips on others. When they avoid important and necessary confrontation with their "moving target" skills or by insisting that "it's not a good time for me to talk about that." In fact, with NFs a relationship can sometimes be wearying. With a few, it can be toxic.

A Final Word

NFs care about people. They have unusual insights about people. They know how to bring out the best in others. They know how to make others feel comfortable and valued. They see the people implications. They are effective communicators. They know how to mobilize and inspire. They are almost always warm, friendly, empathic, and captivating.

NFs—children or adults—make one think of the childhood song:

Playmate, come out and play with me
And bring your dollies three.
Climb up my apple tree,
Holler down my rain barrel,
Slide down my cellar door,
And we'll be jolly friends forever more.

ENFJ

ENFJs make and share judgments about people. They have remarkable gifts at seeing human potential, and they want somehow to contribute to helping others "be the best they can be." More often than not, ENFJs' purpose is altruistic. Sometimes, however, they use their gifts to manipulate others to meet their own needs. Outgoing, sociable, warm, seductive, articulate and often eloquent, ENFJs are often a difficult act to follow. More than any of the other types, they have people charisma. They know how to charm, to soothe, to inspire, or to inflame. Their people-power can be somewhat frightening when they misuse it.

ENFJs often seek opportunities to exercise their people skills in front of audiences. They can be clergy, whose sermons and addresses have unusual dramatic power. They can be teachers who fascinate and entrance their students, who may later wonder why that subject just never was the same with any subsequent teacher. They may be instructors or trainers who invariably find the way to make the course a personal experience for participants. And as public speakers, they give talks that have audiences emotionally engaged—laughing or crying—and hanging on every word.

One ENFJ, for example, was in the midst of an address to hospital administrators. He challenged them about how much they really knew about what was going on in their hospitals.

When," he asked, "was the last time you were in the laundry room talking to your employees there? When was the last time you spoke to the janitorial staff?"

In the room at the time, one of the hotel's janitors was adjusting the air conditioning. He heard every word.

"Right on," mumbled the janitor. He left the room, walked into the hall and pulled the fire alarm. If he couldn't get his manager's attention one way, he'd get it another, the janitor thought!

Many ENFJs have lively senses of humor. They delight in quick quips. They enjoy telling jokes. They have a fund of funny stories to tell about themselves or others. They may even work at remembering them, building up over time a storehouse of amusing anecdotes for almost any occasion. They are very likely to try to establish a connection with an audience by opening a speech with a joke. The response of the audience tells them whether they have succeeded. Most people respond warmly to the ENFJs fund of fun-loving stories. A few are turned off by what they see as an indication of the frivolous nature of ENFJs. And occasionally, ENFJs misjudge an individual or an audience and tell a story that falls flat or receives a cold reception!

An ENFJ secretary is unfailingly polite when handling difficult telephone calls, but as she puts the phone down, she may say with a grin: "Get a job."

At an impromptu get-together after work, someone in her group mentioned blind dates.

"I'm not going on any more blind dates," was her quick comment. "I've been bitten by too many seeing-eye dogs!"

Although audiences turn most ENFJs on, ENFJs have a deep and abiding interest in individuals, too. They look for opportunities to work with and to be of service to others. Despite their warm and supporting nature, ENFJs can be dispassionate and objective. They can be both firm and confrontive when they feel the situation calls for it. Precisely because their general stance is one of warmth and support, when they do criticize, it can seem sharper than it really is. The criticism delivered, ENFJs revert to their "warm-fuzzy" selves. For some, it takes getting used to.

ENFJs for example, may be almost brutal when sharing their judgments with friends and relations. One ENFJ for years paid a ceremonial visit to her brother-in-law and his family at their vacation home. Her message was always the same. Paraphrased, it went like this:

"Hello, I'm so glad to see you again. How have things been? [A little listening and then interrupting at the first opportunity.] Last year, I was in a really bad place emotionally, but this year I'm well. I need to stay away from the rest of the family. I just don't want to get caught up in all the gossiping and storytelling. I'm in a place where I need to be left alone, so please leave me alone. This is just my ceremonial visit for the summer."

Is it any wonder that this ENFJ was not a very popular member of the family?

Another ENFJ occasionally got into trouble when he shared his critical people-centered judgments with friends and family. As a therapist, however, he learned a simple technique that softened what otherwise might have been experienced as a punishing statement. He would begin by saying:

"I'm going to say something to you now. I know it will sound like a judgment, but I want you to hear it just as information. You tell me whether the information fits for you or not and we'll take it from there."

ENFJs have a remarkable sense of how to interest or otherwise have an impact on people. They know how to present information. They know how to market themselves and others. They know how to write material in such a way as to capture the attention of others. They have a flair for catchy titles, phrases, and ways of expressing ideas. Other types can learn a lot from ENFJs about effective communication.

ENFJs' interest in people is so strong that they run the risk of losing themselves in others. They often feel guilty when their efforts to help others do not seem to make a difference. They need to pay attention to the care and feeding of themselves, too. And, despite the pitfalls, for ENFJs that means finding opportunities to do the things they do best—working with people. ENFJs who do not have opportunities to work with and help others can become frustrated, cold, judgmental and withdrawn.

ENFJs' interest in others is so compelling that they run the risk of not giving themselves enough time alone. ENFJs need time alone. When alone they shift from making and expressing judgments about people. They become reflective. They see new possibilities or find new meanings in things. Too much time with others means too many judgments based on limited data.

Nevertheless, some ENFJs avoid being alone. For some reason, these ENFJs find that their focus turns to the darker side of things. They find that when alone they make negative judgments about themselves. Even a few hours alone causes some ENFJs to feel depressed. They, therefore, try to make sure that they fill their waking hours with extraverted things to do. Being with people becomes a way to escape dark thoughts.

ENFJs do not like to make judgments that are strictly impersonal. Logic and analysis is not their long suit. The inner world of abstract thought, as one expert has phrased it, is not for ENFJs. For the most part, they simply do not relate to judgments based on abstract principles applied impersonally. It is a world foreign to them.

Under stress, however, they can become prisoners of logic. They may become extremely critical of themselves or others. They can express bad-tempered judgments and want to hear no challenges to their logic. Cold, indeed, is the ENFJ making and sharing impersonal, logical judgments.

When down on themselves, however, that is exactly what they are likely to do. In particular, they make harsh and impersonal judgments about their contributions to the world. When ENFJs are at their most vulnerable, they withdraw into themselves and turn logic into a weapon against themselves. Is it any wonder, then, that ENFJs who are tearing themselves apart in such a way whenever they are alone are likely to rush out to be with someone else?

Though they would undoubtedly deny it vehemently, a religious career may have a particular attraction for some ENFJs. That part of their work that involves ministering to people makes use of their greatest gifts. Making personal applications of the tenets of their faith also draws upon ENFJ strengths. The theology itself, however, may provide a way to avoid doing that which they do least well—logical, analytical reasoning. They can through faith commit themselves to a theology. By that act of faith they no longer have to deal except by rote with difficult philosophical questions concerning the meaning of life.

While ENFJs can deal with the day-to-day details, it takes real effort and patience on their parts to do so. It does not yield them the satisfaction and pleasure they derive from focusing on possibilities, which more often than not are positive and happy. Many ENFJs, however, so enjoy being organized and orderly that they become meticulous about their homes, their cars, their address and telephone books, or their financial records.

ENFJs are the "teddy-bears" of psychological type. It is seductively easy to get caught up in their warmth, their sense of fun, their belief in others, their contagious enthusiasm. They know how to make others feel comfortable and valued. They know how to draw out even the most introverted of introverts.

Their very skills also make it too easy for others to overlook the fact that ENFJs have needs, too. For they need for themselves what they so generously give to others. They do not, however, often let others know that about themselves. And sometimes, they do not even admit to themselves that they, too, need nourishment and support. Sometimes being the center of attention is a lonely place to be.

INFJ

INFJs are often quietly charming personalities. They are tactful, thoughtful, and concerned for the happiness and welfare of others. They have a gentle graciousness and a soft-spoken persistence that makes them special people for those who know them well. They are artistic, creative, full of penetrating insights, and gifted with the ability to see symbolic meaning in the world around them. They are also deep and complex people, often somewhat puzzling—to themselves as well as to others.

INFJs often possess a curious combination of warmth and distance. They share themselves in their own way at times of their own choosing. Some, for example, demonstrate their warmth through notes, verse, a look, or how they present a gift rather than in physical touching or spoken words. On occasion, INFJs are able—and willing—to break through their customary reserve. They can act light-hearted and even goofy. Seldom, however, will they become boisterous. Frequently, it is the ENFJ who brings out the fun-loving side of INFJs.

Though it is not readily apparent, the driving force in INFJs is an inner focus on possibilities, meanings and relationships about people and values. When alone, they become aware of images, hunches or visions. Though these can be vague and diffuse in nature, they are nonetheless powerful and real to them. They become their guides to action, to future behavior, regardless of what others might say. It is their own inner insights they trust most.

INFJs turn their insights over and over from many different angles. They have what amounts to insights on insights. As a result they can often see the hidden meanings in events or what people do. Their language can be rich in imagery. Many of them find expression for their gifts in creative arts of all kinds. Others become interpreters of the creative arts. Still others turn their talents into understanding people and become outstanding practitioners in the helping professions.

A few move beyond insight into foresight. They become prophets and psychics. They have premonitions about what will happen in the future or what is happening to someone they know who is far away. One INFJ was relieved to learn that this was not an uncommon characteristic of her type. She recalled that she had stopped going to an aerobics class when she had a very strong impression that something was wrong with one of her classmates whom she liked and felt close to. Several months later, she discovered that her friend was seriously ill with cancer.

INFJs are not likely to share with others what takes place inside. Often they could not, even if they wanted to, because the insights are of such an impressionistic nature as to defy articulation. They have a feeling. They cannot put words to it that others can understand. Sharing what goes on inside would make them feel extremely vulnerable. They would feel subject to a kind of external scrutiny they are not prepared to deal with. They only know that their inner impressions are very important, and they accept them as valid.

In part because they have so much faith in their insights, in part because they do not or cannot share them with others, they are sometimes very difficult to understand. They can seem (often are!) extremely stubborn—impervious, almost, to information from others. INFJs may sometimes suffer from their absolute faith in their intuitive insights. They may assume, for example, that they know what someone else is going to say. Rather than let the person complete the thought, they interrupt in the middle of a sentence. Sometimes their assumption is correct. Sometimes it is not. They may find themselves responding to something that the other person wasn't going to say at all. More often than not, however, INFJs' sensitivity to others' feelings causes them to be patient and wait, even if it is for someone to finish the obvious!

INFJs are gentle persons who find conflict particularly destructive. One INFJ father of two young boys who fought a lot with each other made it very clear to his wife that he considered it a sign of their failure as parents whenever the children fought. Years later as president of a local union, he found conflict in the union and between the union and management very unsettling. He began to have chest pains. He thought they were heart attacks and was more than a little surprised when his doctor recommended a quiet drink before dinner.

Even when INFJs assert themselves, they do so in a soft-spoken way. They will confront someone immediately if that's clearly the only way. They prefer to think through a situation carefully. Alone, they plan and rehearse what to say and how to handle themselves. Then they seek out the person or persons they need to talk to. Throughout the encounter, they handle themselves quietly and with restraint—rarely will INFJs raise their voices in real anger. All the while, though, they are likely to feel great emotional turmoil. Confrontations are not the spice of life for INFJs.

Like other introverts, INFJs experience a tension between their inner and outer needs. In their dealings with the external world, they want things organized and orderly. They put a good deal of energy into identifying priorities and plans of action. On the other hand, in their private worlds, they want spontaneity and flexibility. They want to avoid being pinned down to commitments and decisions. Usually neat and orderly, there is often a little piece of their world that reflects anything but systems or order! It can be their desks or studies or some other part of their lives.

INFJs give the appearance of being able to make decisions based on logic and impersonal analysis. Some, for example, pursue science and mathematics and excel at them. The key to their success, however, may not be their logical abilities. What is more likely to be taking place is that their intuitive powers are so great that they see an answer and then work back to how it was that they got there.

INFJs are unusually introspective, and often second guess themselves. Wherever they are in their lives, they may wonder if it's the right place. Should they be doing something else? Are they learning and growing? INFJs can also be quite sure that somehow they have great gifts that they ought to be using, great contributions that they ought to be giving the world. They can get caught between overconfidence on one extreme and doubting themselves on the other. Some INFJs never quite seem to find a peaceful middle ground. Others may never know of the INFJ struggle, for INFJs are private persons. All others see is how the INFJs move through the world with quiet grace.

INFJs' least developed side is the world of the concrete, the world of facts and realities. They can go to extremes when dealing with tasks that are strictly detailed in nature. On the one hand, they may find themselves avoiding realities as long as possible. Then, when they can be avoided no longer, they deal with them with ferocious speed and bad temper. One INFJ on the night of his 50th wedding anniversary watched his ENTP wife begin to open presents. The party was over. Only the children and grandchildren remained. He, who was almost always calm and, indeed, calming, became more and more agitated.

"I don't think you should open these presents now," he said, pacing the room. "We're tired and we won't keep straight which is from whom. We won't know whom to thank for what."

As his wife, enjoying "Christmas" in March, continued to ignore him, he became angry and surprisingly sharp in his statements. Finally, he, who certainly knew how to be organized and make lists, left the room. He went to his study, came out with a pad and pen and marched up to one of his disorganized sons. Shoving the pad and pen at him, he snapped:

"Here, you keep the list. You're the organized one in the family!"

At the other extreme, INFJs become obsessed with details. They see themselves as meticulous and thorough. What they are most often doing, however, is wallowing in facts indiscriminately. They make no sound judgments about which are important and which are not. They can sharply question others about details and be very critical when they do not get satisfactory answers.

When discouraged, INFJs conjure up a host of gloomy and depressing facts about themselves. They may share these details with those close to them. They "yes, but" all attempts to point out that they are being unnecessarily harsh on themselves.

Of all the types, INFJs apparently constitute the smallest percentage in the population. Given the complex nature of their personalities, particularly the unusual quality of their inner world of insights, INFJs may sometimes find life a lonely journey. They may worry too much about who they are and what they and life are all about. Gifted in ways not given to others, they need but to get out of their own way to experience the fullness of their own power.

ENFP

ENFPs are full of warmth, enthusiasm and ingenuity. Intuition is the driving force in their lives. They look about them and see endless possibilities that relate to and involve people. Possibilities excite and energize them. They want to do something about them, and they want to get others involved, too. They are powerfully persuasive when enlisting others in one of their projects. Seductively warm and engaging, ENFPs can charm their way into—or out of—almost anything.

ENFPs follow the possibilities wherever they lead. Over the course of a lifetime, that can mean getting involved in many different interests or careers. ENFPs get asked "when are you going to settle down?" or "what are you going to be when you grow up?" more often than any other type. The question assumes that everyone's life should have a single path, direction or career. Until that happens, one is somehow not quite grown up or mature.

What others fail to see is that ENFPs are quite consistent. From a very early age, they follow their strongly-held intuitive insights wherever they takes them. To others, who see only the changes, ENFPs seem to lack purpose or stability. Not so, and one would be ill-advised to try to force ENFPs into a mold that does not fit them. ENFPs may have the greatest range of interests and abilities of any of the types.

A great challenge for many ENFPs is to learn to discriminate and stick with it long enough to accomplish something. Some give in to the temptation to drop a project half-finished because they see another, more exciting possibility. Those who do not learn to discriminate tend to bounce from one possibility to another, rarely staying with one long enough to see it through to completion. These ENFPs become irresponsible and undependable, and they will squander the gifts they do have.

Many ENFPs examine carefully which of all the exciting possibilities they want to concentrate on. Those who do so and then follow through are often successful in whatever they set out to do. ENFPs make their judgments when alone. That is when they feel the need to sort out what's important and what isn't. That is when they form the value judgments that become important guides to their behavior. ENFPs who do not give themselves time alone can find themselves overwhelmed with too many exciting things to do.

One ENFP is aware that he has more exciting possibilities than he can ever handle. He is equally aware that he needs to complete things. He decides what he will concentrate his energies on and then looks at what it will take to complete a project. If he finds that it will take other people, he uses his knowledge of type and temperament to analyze what kinds of skills he will need. He then systematically identifies and recruits people who have those skills. On more than one occasion, he has turned the actual day-to-day leadership over to someone else. He then plays the role that he believes he is best suited for—and takes great pleasure in how he has used his people skills to create an exciting project team.

Some ENFPs have a high need for approval. ENFPs naturally want to be liked. They want others to say positive things about them. Approval is so important to some that they seek it in subtle and not-so-subtle ways. Often they overdo expressions of warmth and intimacy for others, hoping that others will pick up the message and reflect back similar sentiments. Many of these ENFPs have little sense of self worth. They crave from others what they do not find within themselves. For many of these ENFPs, no amount of approval is enough.

Most ENFPs, however, are genuinely and warmly interested in others. They focus their intuitive skills on understanding and working with people, either individually or in groups. Many ENFPs have unusual people skills. They are quick to sense what makes others "tick." They are sensitive to others' emotional states. They know how to relate to others in ways that are helpful. They are, in short, unusually skillful at bringing out the best in others.

There is sometimes a weak side to ENFPs' people skills. It can manifest itself in a need to be emotionally one-up in relationships. ENFPs, for example, can make effective use of guilt to keep others one-down. If they want something, they may ask for it in a way designed to make others feel guilty unless they grant the request or favor.

Sometimes being one-up in relationships means that ENFPs will pursue someone—or allow themselves to be pursued—until the other person declares himself or herself. At that moment, they lose interest and sometimes reject the very attention they were to that moment encouraging. It is almost as if ENFPs are so intrigued by possibilities that so long as something remains a possibility they want to explore it. The moment it becomes concrete and real, they lose interest. The chase is what's fun. The unknown is fascinating, the known may not be. In short, while most ENFPs are a joy to be around, are warm, responsive and caring individuals, they can sometimes be toxic personalities. They misuse their gifts.

Some ENFPs are masters of the moving-target defense when confronted about their behavior. When criticized for doing or saying something, they either give a rationalization or somehow shift the focus of the conversation. When one accepts what they are now saying and attempts to criticize that position, they shift once again. It becomes almost impossible to pin them down.

While not their strong suit, ENFPs, particularly in the service of an important intuitive insight, can and do make logical judgments. When the situation calls for it, they can analyze impersonally the consequences of things. It is not something that they particularly enjoy doing. Consequently, they may use logic somewhat impatiently.

Facts, realities and the details of life, particularly when unconnected with some exciting possibility, are a real trial for ENFPs. For the most part, they move through life charmingly oblivious to mundane details. When they must focus on details, they can become quickly frustrated and bored. They are likely to develop all kinds of avoidance mechanisms.

Schedules are extremely difficult or confining for some ENFPs. They may not wear watches, or if they do, they may pay little attention to them. They can be late again and again—and always have a dazzling excuse or explanation. One ENFP who travels a great deal estimates that he misses one out of every five flights.

ENFPs may enjoy material things and then fail to do the simplest maintenance. One ENFJ began to notice that the inside of many ENFPs' automobiles looked like what he called "garbage cans on wheels." Like ENTPs, ENFPs are likely not to be sensitive to the needs of their bodies. They can abuse themselves physically and not know it.

Under stress or when discouraged, however, ENFPs will focus on negative details about themselves. They turn inward—become introverted—and find facts that suggest they are unworthy people. They become acutely aware of how they have helped others or how they have served as catalysts to bring out the best in others. But they give themselves no credit for it. They demand specifics to prove to themselves that they have done more than just help others.

For the most part, however, ENFPs live happily and productively in the world of people possibilities. They take great satisfaction in the wide range of their accomplishments. Some work in organizations and find in them the structure and direction that they might not otherwise give themselves. Many others find organizations confining. They do not appreciate the need for following rules, regulations or schedules. Many ENFPs go into lines of work where they can be their own bosses and follow their own schedules. Gifted, sensitive, creative, gregarious, spontaneous, people-oriented, there seems no end of exciting things for ENFPs to be and do.

INFP

INFPs find their deepest meaning in life when they can contribute to the creation of a better world for all people. And what INFPs want more than anything else is to identify for themselves what their own "deepest meaning" is. What path will they take with their lives? To what will they devote their talents, skills and energy? Only a few INFPs need to manage organizations. Seldom do they seek to be the center of attention. They want to be able to work quietly—often unobtrusively—for what is their life's quest.

INFPs are people oriented. They focus on human potential, and they base their decisions on a careful and thorough—often painstaking—weighing of values. What matters? What should matter? What are the most important, the most enduring, values? What represents the best, the purest thing to do? How can I make the most valued contribution? These are the considerations that INFPs focus on when alone, and from their inner values come the guidance for their lives.

Those who are close to INFPs see their flexibility and adaptability. They see the ease with which INFPs generate intuitive insights about people. What others are not so likely to see is the powerful inner drive to turn those insights into decisions—into plans for the betterment of mankind. INFPs know, if others don't, that the key to their personalities is the search for values that will provide direction in their lives. They take in data about people-possibilities. They want to know how they can contribute to bringing out the best in others. They have visions about a more humane world. They want to be a part of bringing about that better world. The desire is a very deeply rooted one in INFPs. They are at their happiest when involved in work that has social value.

Although it may not be readily apparent, many INFPs are shy and private people. Some show it by their somewhat reserved and "proper" manner, particularly in the beginning of relationships. Some seem more outgoing—they have usually prepared themselves and rehearsed their extraverted behavior. One young INFP prepared herself for her dates by thinking of questions to ask her young man to keep him talking about himself. Then she wrote the questions down, memorized them and put the list in her pocketbook! Other INFPs turn extraverted activities into acting roles to play. They find in the thought that they are role-playing the confidence they need to project an outgoing image.

INFPs have the ability to put people at ease. They are almost always thoughtful, gracious, and considerate. They are genuinely interested in people and sensitive to where others are "coming from." What others experience with INFPs is their people orientation and their depth of caring. In their own quiet ways, INFPs are warm personalities. The better they get to know others, the more the warmth and caring shows.

INFPs are often gifted writers, able to turn their gracious ways into graceful prose, poetry or song. Any awkwardness they may feel in extraverted speaking roles disappears when they write. When they put in writing their innermost thoughts and feelings, they identify personally with the product. They can easily become very sensitive to others' reactions to it.

Publicly sharing their deepest values, no matter how they have rehearsed themselves, is difficult. They feel exposed and vulnerable. They can, however, be powerful public speakers. Their audiences cannot help but hear the depth of their commitment through the content of their remarks. Their vulnerability shows and often captures the attention and emotions of their audiences.

INFPs often undervalue themselves. They set extremely high standards and measure themselves against them, regardless of how impressed others are with their work. They only care about whether they are living up to their inner ideals. The phrase "it is only when viewed against their promise that their record looks so bleak" may have particular meaning for many INFPs. Some INFPs never resolve the conflict between their high internal expectations of themselves and the demands of day-to-day living. Those who don't resolve the conflict can become weak, ineffective and even paralyzed personalities.

INFPs' high standards can hurt them in another way as well. They measure the finished product against standards of perfection. Their need to have everything just right sometimes makes them unwilling to let go or to delegate responsibility. Control needs constitute the Achilles heel of more than a few INFPs.

Many INFPs are genuinely puzzled or hurt when told they have control needs. They prefer Isabel Myers' description: INFPs are "open-minded, flexible and adaptable—until one of the things they value most deeply seems in danger—at which point they stop adapting." Myers, an INFP herself, could not help but describe what many experience as control needs in the best possible light! "The iron fist in the velvet glove" is a less gentle but very apt phrase to describe INFPs when they become protective of what they value.

INFPs do not like conflict, and many will go to great lengths to avoid it. Oftentimes INFPs' first reaction is to withdraw deep into their shells, like turtles, to avoid confrontation. If withdrawal is not an appropriate response, some INFPs will first spend time alone to prepare themselves. Thus prepared, they will discuss what needs to be discussed. All in all, however, they'd rather avoid it.

When INFPs do address interpersonal problems, their impulse is to focus on their emotional reaction to what others have said or done. Their feelings, not the rightness or wrongness of what happened, is the important thing. Interestingly, many INFPs have an unusual ability to help others resolve conflict. They can put to good use their desire for harmony and their sensitivity to their own and others' feelings.

In the pursuit of an important value, INFPs can be persistently and meticulously concerned about details. They can painstakingly collect needed data. They will work and rework details, always striving to meet the high standards they set for themselves. Details unconnected with projects that are important to them are quite another matter. Some are frustratingly or charmingly in another world with regard to the details of daily living.

INFPs' least developed side is logic and impersonal analysis. They do not like to make decisions based on looking at the impersonal "if-then" consequences of things. When operating at their best, they form conclusions logically or analytically. Under stress, however, INFPs may lash out with impersonal, analytical judgments rigidly expressed and dogmatically held. They race through a great deal of data, often misstating it. They examine hastily what strikes them as the logical implications. Then, they express their conclusions with strong hostile emotions.

One INFP lawyer (an unusual profession for an INFP precisely because legal judgments are supposed to be impersonal and logical, not value and person centered) was attending a workshop on type. She was a silent participant until thinking and feeling judgments were defined and explained. At that point, she became both vocal and hostile. She absolutely could not accept the distinction between the two. She argued with and misquoted the trainer. She attempted to show how the distinctions were logically invalid. When the trainer pointed out that he had not said or implied what she heard, she fell quiet for a few moments. Then she erupted again, saying virtually the same thing a second time. By the third repetition of this conversation, it finally became clear to the trainer that the discussion had caused the INFP participant to become locked into her least developed side—and she was captured by it, caught in its negative power.

Sometimes, INFPs use logic as a weapon against themselves. When lost in low self-esteem, they set up "if. . .then" statements that can only lead to the conclusion that they have not accomplished anything worth accomplishing. They logically conclude that their lives have had little meaning or value. They incorporate the high standards they set for themselves into negative and logical self criticism.

Fortunately, INFPs usually operate out of the better developed sides of their type. They make effective use of their ability to see human potential and to identify for themselves and others the most important, positive and enduring values. INFPs are probably the most idealistic of all types. In the pursuit of their ideals, they drive themselves harder and judge themselves more critically than any other type. Through their lives and through their work, they seek to contribute to a better world for us all. Their determination and drive, expressed with quiet and gentle grace, often enable them to achieve far more than they are willing to give themselves credit for.

VI Temperament and the World of Work

Each of the four sets of preferences yields important insights into human behavior. Different pairs of preferences give us additional useful insights. The temperament pairs (SJ, SP, NT, NF) are particularly powerful, for they identify important behavior patterns and belief structures. The temperament pairing also has practical advantages. Often the sixteen types provide so much information that it is difficult to use effectively. In the classroom, for example, trying to develop curriculums that appeal to sixteen different types is a formidable task. To focus one's attention on four temperaments, however, is much more manageable.

In the same way, keeping sixteen distinctions in mind in the world of work can be overwhelming for busy managers. Again, the temperament pairings provide managers with a practical and powerful tool. Managing means getting things done through others. To be effective at that task requires understanding of self and others, knowing how to match the right person with the right job, and helping people to work together to accomplish organizational goals. Knowledge of temperament can help managers do these things.

The chart on the following pages provides an outline of the differing gifts each temperament brings to the world of work.

VII Temperaments in the World of Work

Name:	Visionaries (NT)	Catalysts (NF)	Trouble-Shooter/Negotiators (SP)	Traditionalist/Stabilizers (SJ)
Look At The World And See:	Possibilities, meanings and relationships	Possibilities, meanings and relationships	Facts and realities	Facts and realities
And Want To:	Examine their consequences analytically, impersonally.	Judge their value to people and for people.	Collect more, manipulate facts and realities.	Organize facts and realities.
They Have A Life-long Drive For:	Competence and knowledge	Meaning, authenticity, identity.	Action, excitement, competition.	Contributing to meaningful social institutions.
And Thus They Are Effective:	As architects of change, as organizational entrepreneurs.	In getting people to work effectively together to achieve organizational goals.	In crisis situations, in pulling "the fat out of the fire," producing results.	As stabilizers of organizations, as maintainers of traditions.
Their Strengths Include:	• Looking ahead, seeing new possibilities. • Conceptualizing, designing especially with regard to organizational change. • Setting high standards, particularly intellectually. • Seeing right to the heart of complex issues or problems. • Seeing the large picture, the larger context. • Grasping the underlying principles, dynamics, laws. • At their best when someone says "it can't be done."	• Drawing out the best in people. • Working with and through people—participative leadership. • Good verbal *and* listening skills. • Being sensitive to the organizational climate. • Expressing empathy. • Being creative. • Getting people to work effectively and harmoniously together. • Learning new things, particularly about self and others.	• Handling crisis situations. • Seeing what's negotiable. • Being ingenious and re-sourceful getting things done. • Knowing how to expedite things. • Being honest and straight-forward—"telling it like it is." • Having a practical approach to concrete problems. • Being adaptable, flexible. • Taking risks.	• Being realistic and practical. • Being decisive. • Paying attention to rules, policies and regulations. • Bringing a planned, organized approach to work. • Being dependable, steady workers, good at following through • Being thorough, systematic and precise, especially with details.
Their Potential Weaknesses:	• Do not easily show sensitivity and appreciation to others • Not following through on details—getting bored routine. • Can lose people with their fascination for complexity. • Elitist • Impatient with those whom they don't see as competent.	• Being too generous giving of time and self to others. • Deciding on the basis of personal likes and dislikes. • Giving too much autonomy and freedom. • Being too easily hurt— • Placing too much focus on people, not enough on organizational goals. • Having trouble "biting the bullet" especially when it may mean hurting people.	• Disliking, being impatient with the theoretical, the abstract, the conceptual. • Being unpredictable. • Becoming bored when there no crises to solve. • Creating crises to have something exciting to do. • Producing written documents. • Not taking a stand, seeming indecisive. • Being impulsive—not looking before they leap.	• Not always being responsive to the need for change. • Being a "rule is a rule is a rule/if I made an exception for you I'd have to make an exception for everybody" person. • Deciding things too quickly. • Being impatient with delays and complications. • Having an excessive concern for crises that may never occur.

Name:	Visionaries (NT)	Catalysts (NF)	Trouble-Shooter/Negotiators (SP)	Traditionalist/Stabilizers (SJ)
Their Contributions In A Work Team Include:	• Tracking thought processes. • Problem solving. • Providing theoretical input. • Contagious enthusiasm for ideas.	• Adding the personal dimension. • Selling the organization or cause they believe in. • Bringing out the contributions of others.	• Making things happen. • Spotting practical problems. • Negotiating agreements or plans of action.	• Focusing on what needs to be done. • Focusing on follow through. • Focusing on important details.
They Like To Be Appreciated For:	The quality of their ideas and their intellectual competency.	Themselves as people who make important contributions.	The clever way they make things happen or get things done.	Their careful, thorough, accurate work.
They Provide:	Idea charisma	People charisma	Crisis charisma	Relief from charisma!
Their Motto Might Be:	*"Some men see things as they are and say why, I dream things that never were and say why not?"* Robert F. Kennedy	*"This above all: to thine own self be true And it must follow, as night the day, Thou canst not then be false to any man."* William Shakespeare, *Hamlet*	*"Damn the torpedoes, full speed ahead."* David Farragut, Battle of Mobile Bay, 1863	*"Neither rain nor snow, nor sleet, nor dark of night shall stay the courier from the swift completion of his appointed rounds."* Post Office motto

VIII   How the Temperaments Relate

Sensing gives SJs and SPs some common characteristics, just as intuition builds bridges between NTs and NFs. There are, however, some unusual relationship patterns among the four temperaments:

- SJs and NFs can have an unusual empathy for one another.
- SPs and NTs can develop mutual warmth and respect.
- SJs and NTs frequently clash.
- SPs and NFs often have real difficulty appreciating each other.

The empathy that SJs and NFs have for each other has to do with their respective basic drives. SJs have a life-long need to belong and contribute to meaningful social institutions. NFs have a life-long drive for identity. SJs cannot express their need for belonging without developing an awareness of their own identity. Belonging, after all, means fitting in, and fitting in means having some sense of self. NFs, in turn, cannot search for their own identity in a vacuum. Thus for them, identity usually means being concerned about belonging. In one sense, the basic drives of SJs and NFs are like two sides of the same coin.

The mutual respect that SPs and NTs have for one another also involves their basic drives. SPs thrive on action, activity and competition. Being active develops competence and often generates respect for those who care about competence. The NT drive is for competence—and developing their competence means that they often put themselves into competitive situations. Thus, NTs often respect the SP's competitiveness. Competition is a means to an end for NTs. For SPs, competence is a means to an end. Again, it's like two sides of the same coin.

The clash that often exists between SJs and NTs has to do with tradition and authority. SJs respect authority, and they believe that others should respect them when they are in positions of authority. They do not understand people who rebel against authority, and they may, in fact, be quite critical of those who do so. NTs, on the other hand, are the visionary temperament. They are the architects of change. As they think of new ways of doing things and new things to do, they do not appreciate being told SJ things like: "What do you want to do that for? What's the matter with the way we do it now?" Or, "if it ain't broke, don't fix it." Or, "a rule is a rule is a rule. If I broke it for you I'd have to break it for everyone else."

With SPs and NFs the clash comes around action and identity, activity and introspection. SPs define their own identity through action. Action is what counts, not identity. They do not understand all the soul-searching, the quest for meaning, that goes with the NF territory. SPs often get impatient with NFs. They think NFs are mush-heads talking nonsense. NFs would much rather appreciate people than be critical of them. They are more often than not hurt by SPs' failure to understand them. The action of SPs seems pointless, frenetic, purposeless. To NFs, SPs have little or no sense of self.

These are the important temperament-related differences that are not quickly apparent. Understanding them can help people of different temperaments build bridges, not walls, between themselves and others.

I   Introduction

Most people, when first introduced to type and temperament theories, want to know what the terms mean. They want to read about themselves. Having done that, a common reaction is: "Wow, is this interesting! It's just like reading a horoscope!" And a few ask if there is any relationship between what they've just read and astrology. For many people, much of the information is unusually accurate. It doesn't seem possible that these four simple preferences could yield so much detailed information.

By themselves, they don't. Jung had a specific formula to describe how the preferences combine to form a whole. The preferences interact in prescribed patterns. It is the way the parts combine that explains much of the behavior of each type. The whole is, indeed, far greater than the sum of its parts!

Knowing Jung's formula is important for those who want to make the fullest use of knowledge of type theory. Without that knowledge, we cannot go beyond the preferences and the written descriptions. Knowing how the preferences combine explains the material in the descriptions. It enables us to go beyond them. It provides us with the tools to understand behavior in ways that the definitions of the preferences and the descriptions cannot. It makes dynamic and flexible a theory that would otherwise be static and limited. So . . . , if we want to go beyond the horoscope, we must learn how the preferences combine!

II   Back to the Preferences

The first chapter emphasized the either/or nature of Jung's theory. It focuses more on the polarities. We are either:

extraverts or introverts
sensing or intuitive
thinking or feeling
judging or perceiving

In this chapter, we will revisit the preferences from the both/and perspective. We will be emphasizing that we have all the preferences in us:

Key Point:

We all have extraverted and introverted tendencies.

We all use sensing and intuition.

We all make thinking and feeling judgments.

We all have judging and perceiving needs.

III Attitudes and Functions

Key Points:

1. The second and third sets of preferences (sensing and intuition, thinking and feeling) are called "functions". They describe different ways by which we collect information and make decisions.

   Sensing and intuition are the functions of perception. They deal with how we perceive things.

   Thinking and feeling are the functions of judgment. They describe two different ways by which we form judgments, decisions and conclusions.

2. The first and fourth sets of preferences (extraversion and introversion, judging and perceiving) are called "attitudes". In the sense that we will be talking about them in this chapter, they do not stand alone. They define how each type uses the functions. They describe how the functions combine.

To understand how the preferences combine, it is important to keep in mind which sets of preferences are functions and which are attitudes. The two groups of preferences play quite different roles in shaping each psychological type:

- The middle sets of preferences—the functions—constitute the core of each type. The four functions interact in each type according to prescribed patterns.

- The first and fourth sets of preferences tell us how.

Functions: Think of functions as mental processes. They are the tools we use to collect information and make decisions.

- Sensing collects information about specifics.

- Intuition generates information about meanings, possibilities and relationships.

- Thinking makes decisions that are logical, impersonal and analytical.

- Feeling makes decisions by arranging things in accordance with their value to us. Feeling judgments are sensitive to our own and others' feelings.

Because sensing and intuition are mental processes by which we collect and generate information, Jung called them the "perceiving functions."

Because both thinking and feeling are mental processes by which we make judgments and decisions, Jung called them the "judging functions."

We all use these functions all the time. Often situations demand that we use one of them. When that happens, we can do it. It is, of course, easier for us to use our preferred functions. But we can and do make use of all the functions.

Attitudes: The first and fourth sets of preferences are called attitudes. In the first chapter, the definitions, dialogues and summary charts emphasized the behavioral characteristics that go with each preference. Extraversion/ introversion and judging/perceiving also serve another purpose. They show how the functions combine in different ways in each of the sixteen types.

IV   How the Parts Combine: An Overview

Key Point:

A function is either extraverted or introverted.

> We all deal with the world around us. We use one of our preferred functions when we are dealing with the world outside us. We extravert one of our preferred functions.

> We all have an inner world. We use the other preferred function when we focus on the world inside us. We introvert the other of our preferred functions.

Though authorities differ, the evidence suggests that it is the same with the functions that are less well developed. One of them is extraverted. The other is introverted.

Key Point:

The two preferred functions form a team.

> In each type, one of the preferred functions dominates—it is the "boss" of that type. It is the "dominant" function.

> The other function serves as a loyal subordinate—it is the "auxiliary" function. It supports the dominant function.

Psychological type theory reflects the fact that much of what we do is to collect information and make decisions. One of our preferred functions describes what kind of information we like to collect and how. The other preferred function defines how we like to make judgments. To be effective personalities, these two functions need to work closely together, but one needs to be "in charge". The other needs to be a strong support to it.

Key Point:

Our less developed functions have a place in our personalities, too.

> One is our least developed function. We often have little or no control over it, and it frequently makes trouble for us. It is our "inferior" function.

> The other, though not well developed, we have more control over. It doesn't have a "real" name—it is referred to as the "third" or tertiary function!

Think of it this way: We all take in sensing data, and we all make intuitive leaps. We make both thinking and feeling judgments all the time. The problem is that all that is too much for our conscious minds to handle. So, if we prefer sensing to intuition, we let the intuitive data slide by our awareness. We concentrate our energy on the information our sensing provides. If we prefer thinking judgments to feeling judgments, we are more sensitive to and make conscious use of our thinking function. We ignore or pay scant attention to our feeling judgments. Our third and inferior functions are the ones that we do not pay much attention to. We don't use them as often or as well as we do our dominant and auxiliary functions.

Summary:

Each function is either extraverted or introverted, and each is either dominant, auxiliary, third or inferior. For those who remember their English grammar, each function has two modifiers!

Each type has its own distinctive combination of functions. No two are exactly alike. This is how the functions combine in each of the sixteen types:

There are four types whose dominant is sensing.

For two of them, sensing is both dominant and extraverted.

ESTP	sensing:	extraverted	and	dominant
	thinking:	introverted	and	auxiliary
	intuition:	introverted	and	inferior
	feeling:	extraverted	and	third
ESFP	sensing:	extraverted	and	dominant
	feeling:	introverted	and	auxiliary
	intuition:	introverted	and	inferior
	thinking:	extraverted	and	third

For two of them sensing is dominant and introverted.

ISTJ	sensing:	introverted	and	dominant
	thinking:	extraverted	and	auxiliary
	intuition:	extraverted	and	inferior
	feeling:	introverted	and	third
ISFJ	sensing:	introverted	and	dominant
	feeling:	extraverted	and	auxiliary
	intuition:	extraverted	and	inferior
	thinking:	introverted	and	third

There are four types whose dominant is intuition.

For two of them, intuition is dominant and extraverted.

ENTP	intuition:	extraverted	and	dominant
	thinking:	introverted	and	auxiliary
	sensing:	introverted	and	inferior
	feeling:	extraverted	and	third
ENFP	intuition:	extraverted	and	dominant
	feeling:	introverted	and	auxiliary
	sensing:	introverted	and	inferior
	thinking:	extraverted	and	third

For two of them, intuition is dominant and introverted.

INTJ	intuition:	introverted	and	dominant
	thinking:	extraverted	and	auxiliary
	sensing:	extraverted	and	inferior
	feeling:	introverted	and	third

INFJ	intuition:	introverted	and	dominant
	feeling:	extraverted	and	auxiliary
	sensing:	extraverted	and	inferior
	thinking:	introverted	and	third

There are four types whose dominant is thinking.

For two of them, thinking is dominant and extraverted.

ESTJ	sensing:	introverted	and	auxiliary
	thinking:	extraverted	and	dominant
	intuition:	extraverted	and	third
	feeling:	introverted	and	inferior

ENTJ	intuition:	introverted	and	auxiliary
	thinking:	extraverted	and	dominant
	sensing:	extraverted	and	**third**
	feeling:	introverted	and	inferior

For two of them, thinking is dominant and introverted.

ISTP	sensing:	extraverted	and	auxiliary
	thinking:	introverted	and	dominant
	intuition:	introverted	and	third
	feeling:	extraverted	and	inferior

INTP	intuition:	extraverted	and	auxiliary
	thinking:	introverted	and	dominant
	sensing:	introverted	and	third
	feeling:	extraverted	and	inferior

There are four types whose dominant is feeling.

For two of them, feeling is dominant and extraverted.

ESFJ	sensing:	introverted	and	auxiliary
	feeling:	extraverted	and	dominant
	intuition:	extraverted	and	third
	thinking:	introverted	and	inferior

ENFJ	intuition:	introverted	and	auxiliary
	feeling:	extraverted	and	dominant
	sensing:	extraverted	and	third
	thinking:	introverted	and	inferior

For two of them, feeling is dominant and introverted.

ISFP	sensing:	extraverted	and	auxiliary
	feeling:	introverted	and	dominant
	intuition:	introverted	and	third
	thinking:	extraverted	and	inferior

INFP	intuition:	extraverted	and	auxiliary
	feeling:	introverted	and	dominant
	sensing:	introverted	and	third
	thinking:	extraverted	and	inferior

So what? What does all that mean? How can it help to better understand our own and others' behavior?

V When A Function Is Dominant . . .

When a function dominates our behavior, it exercises control over and provides direction for that type. It is the "boss" of that personality.

- When sensing is dominant, information about specifics is the driving force of type. Collecting concrete data is what these types do best. They are deeply invested in the facts and realities that their sensing function collects. They have the greatest trust in information their sensing function provides them. Sensing gives direction to their lives.

- When intuition is dominant, information about meanings, possibilities, patterns and relationships is the driving force of type. Generating that kind of information comes naturally to these types, and they are very good at it. They are most energized when involved in activities that require intuitive skills. Intuitive insights govern their lives.

- When thinking is dominant, logical, analytical and impersonal judgments are the driving force of type. Forming and acting on thinking judgments gives direction to the behavior of these types. Those for whom thinking is the dominant function are at their best when engaged in activities that require thinking judgments.

- When feeling is dominant, judgments that involve sorting out and applying personal values are the driving force. Those for whom feeling is the dominant function are particularly comfortable in situations calling for judgments that require arranging things in accordance with their value. They are at their best in situations that call for sensitivity to others. Feeling judgments guide their lives.

Each of us needs a dominant function. Why is this so? Why must one of our preferred functions be dominant? If our preferred functions were equal, we'd be constantly confused as to whether we want to collect information or make decisions. We would be, to use a phrase of Isabel Myers, "like ships without a rudder." We would be like a car without a driver, a plane without a pilot, a football team without a quarterback. Each type, therefore, must have a dominant function. Without one, the personality is directionless.

VI What the Auxiliary Adds

If the dominant function gives direction to the personality, then the auxiliary provides essential balance. Those whose dominant is either sensing or intuition need to have a balancing judging function. It can be either thinking or feeling. Without a strong auxiliary judging function, these personalities will move from one thing to another, from one fascinating piece of information to another. They will be impulsive, unpredictable, unstable. They may say they are going to do something but will rarely do much more than start. They may set a date and never show up. Or they may arrive late with all kinds of excuses.

What is happening with these people? They are so involved in whatever information seems exciting at the moment that they cannot seem to make judgments or decisions. They are what we often refer to as the "flakes" of the world. They lack the stability and the balance that an auxiliary judging function would give them. It is the judging function that says: "Hey, enough information. What are you going to do with it?"

Those whose dominant function is a judging one, either thinking or feeling, need good information on which to base their decisions. Either sensing or intuition can provide it. Those who lack a balancing auxiliary function to provide good data are rigid personalities. They are the ones for whom the statement was made: "My mind is made up. Don't confuse me with the facts!" They believe they got long ago almost all the information they need to make decisions. They get one small scrap of information, and they have *the* answer ready. Often they sound like a broken record that simply repeats again and again the same formula to almost any given situation. What they need is an auxiliary function that will say: "Hey, wait a minute. Wait until you have some real information upon which to base that judgment!"

We'll talk about the third and inferior functions later.

VII Extraverted and Introverted Functions

Sometimes it is useful to think of the functions as languages. One of our preferred functions is the language we speak when we are dealing with others. We switch to our other preferred function when we begin to carry on a private conversation with ourselves. That is what it means to extravert one of our preferred functions and introvert the other. We are more comfortable dealing with the outside world with one of our functions and using the other when we are alone. The same principles hold true for our less preferred functions—we extravert one and we introvert the other.

How do we know that we extravert one function and introvert the other? By listening! Some people consistently speak the language of judgments. They move conversations toward closure, and they share their own judgments easily and quickly. They often get impatient with those who seem to avoid declaring themselves. Their behavior changes when it comes to sharing information. They are likely to fall silent or to ask questions to collect information, rather than sharing their information directly. If one could get inside their minds one would find that when alone, they shift languages and begin to focus on information.

A group of people, all of whom extravert their thinking function, for example, trade conclusions. To them, the purpose of discussing something is to make a judgment about it. As they each share judgments, they may find themselves in quick agreement. If not, they may begin to compromise. Sometimes, however, the discussion will turn into an argument. Each of the participants is saying to the others: "my judgment is better than yours!" Such discussions-turned-arguments can degenerate into each restating his or her judgment—louder—with no one listening to anyone else.

Not all types deal with others through the language of judgments. Other types prefer to share information. Their conversations are characterized by an easy, spontaneous flow of information. They want to open conversations up—to explore all kinds of information. Watch, for example, a group of people all of whom extravert intuition! Don't look for them to have a discussion that stays focused! They wander all over the place. Their conversations have many unexpected turns as one possibility suggests another . . . and another . . . and another.

To the trained observer, it's often amusing to watch the struggle that can take place between those who extravert their preferred judging function and those who extravert their preferred perceiving function. The former try to drive the latter to form a judgment, to come to closure. The latter try to keep the former discussing information.

The fact that one of our preferred functions is extraverted and the other is introverted does not mean that we never cross over. Those who extravert their preferred judging function do sometimes share information. When they do, though, they are likely to do so tentatively—almost awkwardly. It's as if they feel a little bit exposed or unsure of themselves. They are likely to share their judgments and then give the information in back of it. And, often, given a few moments alone, they'll suddenly become aware of the other relevant information and wonder why they did not think of it at the time. They may wonder: "Why didn't I think of that then?"

Those who extravert their preferred perceiving function sometimes do express judgments. Their judgments, however, are almost always expressed hypothetically—guardedly. They state judgments in such a way as to leave themselves open to change them if new data comes along. Asked a question that requires them to respond with a judgment and they are likely to hesitate. They talk about the data that they believe is relevant to the decision being discussed. Inside, their minds are busy forming a judgment. If as they share information, their judgment becomes clear, they may say something like this: "So, it seems to me that it all adds up to . . . ," at which point they— finally— take a stand. Often, even a few moments alone is enough to allow them to see much more clearly what their conclusion is. They may then wonder why it wasn't obvious when they were talking. They may wonder why they could not get right to the point. They, too, may wish they could have the conversation over again.

It is important to remember that those types that extravert their preferred judging function introvert their preferred perceiving function. When with others, they are conclusion driven. When alone, they focus on information.

On the other hand, those who extravert their preferred perceiving function introvert their preferred judging function. When these types are with others, they happily discuss information. When alone, they figure out what it all means. Alone, their minds turn to forming conclusions.

We all need to collect information. We all need to decide things. We all prefer to do one of these things when we are with others. We prefer to do the other internally.

VIII Putting the Two Together
Dominant and Auxiliary Functions
Extraverted and Introverted Functions

When we put together the fact that each type has a dominant function and that each function must be either extraverted or introverted in its orientation, we find that there are eight possible dominant functions:

extraverted sensing
introverted sensing

extraverted intuition
introverted intuition

extraverted thinking
introverted thinking

extraverted feeling
introverted feeling

The dominant function and its extraverted or introverted orientation governs much of the behavior of each type. (The auxiliary function and its orientation defines further the dynamics of each of the sixteen types.)

Because the differences are so marked between dominant functions that are extraverted and introverted and because so much of the behavior of each type is governed by its dominant function and its orientation, it is often helpful to describe briefly what these combinations look like:

- ESTPs and ESFPs are the two types for whom sensing is dominant and extraverted. They want to relate to the "real" world as it is happening right now. They focus on the specifics of the moment or situation at hand. They are the supreme realists, the opportunists, of type. They want to do things, to be active. They take pleasure in and are absorbed with the world as it unfolds before them. The world of ESTPs is a more impersonal one than that of ESFPs, whose feeling makes them more sensitive to people and their emotions.

- ISTJs and ISFJs are the two types for whom sensing is dominant and introverted. They want to reflect upon inner realities. They store in their minds vast quantities of details about the world and, when alone, review them. That triggers sensations inside them—other sets of details. It is these details that become the important guides of their lives. To identify and accept these inner realities and to live lives consistent with them is the key for introverted sensing types. Thus, of all the types, they become characterized by super-dependability—they are the responsibility people. For ISTJs, the important realities are more impersonal; for ISFJs the important realities are those that center on serving people.

- ENTPs and ENFPs are the two types for whom intuition is dominant and extraverted. They want to be free to see possibilities in the world around them. They want to be free to follow where those possibilities lead. They are the ingenious types, drawn power fully to that next world to conquer. ENTPs are more conceptually oriented. ENFPs are more people centered.

- INTJs and INFJs are the two types for whom intuition is dominant and introverted. Seeing inner meanings in things is what gives them direction and purpose. Introverted intuitives store all kinds of insights about the external world. When alone they look at them from many different angles. They see new and more ingenious possibilities and meanings as they turn the data over in their minds. They are type's mystics. Because the intuitions that are important to them come from the inner recesses of their minds without system or order and because their intuitive impressions are often vague, others can find them hard to understand. Puzzling or not, however, introverted intuitives will strive to make their internal insights living realities. The inner visions of INTJs are more architectural, conceptual and impersonal. INFJs focus their insights on people and values.

- ESTJs and ENTJs are the two types for whom thinking is dominant and extraverted. They want to "run as much of the world as is theirs to run," to use Myers' phrase. They want to organize their external world by making and following through on logical judgments about it. As Keirsey suggests, they are the "commandants" of type. ESTJs focus their organizing energies more on a world of details and specifics, ENTJs on broader, more strategic considerations.

- ISTPs and INTPs are the two types for whom thinking is dominant and introverted. They want, again quoting Myers, to "understand the world, not run it." They want to organize and make logical judgments about patterns of thought. Introverted thinkers are the philosophers and theorists of type. Of the two types, ISTPs are more practical and application oriented. INTPs more speculative and abstract.

- ESFJs and ENFJs are the two types for whom feeling is dominant and extraverted. They make value judgments about people. They focus their attention on others and like to share affirming value judgments about them. They are most fulfilled when they can bring warmth, support and harmony to their worlds. They are the harmonizing types. ESFJs focus on the details they see about people. ENFJs focus on the potential they see in individuals or groups.

- ISFPs and INFPs are the two types for whom feeling is dominant and introverted. They want to identify, define and sort out the values that reflect the best of humankind. They want to live by those values and thereby make the most meaningful contribution possible. They are the conscience-driven types. ISFPs, shaped by their sensing, work out their innermost values in ways that are specific and concrete. INFPs are more likely to focus their energies in areas having to do with human potential.

Jung believed, then, that extraversion and introversion combine with a dominant function to provide us with keys to understanding and appreciating individual differences. In fact, he so focused on the importance of the dominant function and its extraverted or introverted orientation that he only wrote descriptions of eight pairs of types. He did recognize that there were sixteen types, but he thought that the eight pairs had so much in common as to warrant only eight descriptions. Indeed, the names he gave the eight pairs reflect how important he thought these aspects of his type theory were. To him, there were:

extraverted sensing types
introverted sensing types

extraverted intuitives
introverted intuitives

extraverted thinkers
introverted thinkers

extraverted feeling types
introverted feeling types

IX The Underdeveloped Functions

Now we need to return to an important point we raised at the beginning of this chapter. We all use all the functions all the time. We need to talk about our less well developed functions, for they, too, play important roles in each psychological type.

Most of us at one time or another have had fun trying to push a big ball under the water. The deeper we try to push it, the more it tries to come out from under our hands. The deeper we are able to push it before it slips away, the more forcefully does it burst up from underneath the water. The functions are a little like that. As we use one function, we push its opposite away from our conscious minds. Because one of our preferred functions is our most used, its opposite is the least used. In other words, when one function dominates, its opposite is powerfully repressed.

The opposite of our dominant function, then, is our least developed function. It is the one that, when out of control like our ball in the pool, erupts with great force. Jung called that function our inferior function. Thus:

If sensing is dominant, then intuition is inferior.

If intuition is dominant, then sensing is inferior.

If thinking is dominant, then feeling is inferior.

If feeling is dominant, then thinking is inferior.

When does the inferior function express itself? When does it, like the beach ball, get out of control? It is most likely to do so when:

- We are tired, run down, or ill.

- We are under stress.

- We are under the influence of drugs or alcohol.

- We are with intimate friends or relations.

- We are depressed or down on ourselves.

- We dream.

Given this list of conditions under which the inferior function is likely to burst forth, is it any wonder that this function is an important one, that it plays an important role in each type? Clearly, the inferior function is a key ingredient in understanding our own and other's behavior.

There are several important things to keep in mind about the inferior function:

1. There are times when we can consciously access our inferior function. When that happens, we are in charge. The inferior function is not in charge of us. But it is not easy. We feel awkward, we make mistakes, and we need to be patient with ourselves. In short, we are not comfortable or skilled when we use the inferior function, but we can do it.

2. When the control that our conscious minds exerts over us weakens and our inferior function bursts forth, it is in control of us, not we of it.

3. If the dominant is extraverted, then the inferior will be introverted. If the dominant is introverted, the inferior will be extraverted. (Pity the poor introvert! Extraverts show the world their most powerful function and keep their least developed function to themselves. Introverts do the opposite.)

4. The inferior function expresses itself in either positive or negative extremes:

   - Inferior sensing manifests itself by focusing on excessively (and often unrealistically!) morbid details or on equally unrealistically happy ones.

- Inferior intuition generates totally unrealistically positive predictions or equally totally unrealistically negative predictions.

- Inferior thinking races through logic to come up with angry, depressive conclusions, or ones that lead to unrealistic euphoria.

- Inferior feeling focuses on value judgments that support a depressive self-image or it can manifest itself in an outpouring of love or sentimentality—as often as not inappropriately!

5. Paradoxical as it may seem, the inferior function is both our enemy and our friend. It is our enemy in the sense that when in control of us, it may lead us to do things that are not wise or helpful. It is our friend in the sense that it brings to our conscious minds—if we are willing to listen—messages from another (and important) part of ourselves. An example:

A man for whom feeling was the inferior function found himself powerfully drawn to a much younger person. Disturbed by his feelings for this young person, he asked himself what was the meaning of the attraction? At first, he thought it was because the younger person was a "free spirit" child, someone whose free spirit could be a source of great strength and beauty. The world, he thought, does not appreciate free spirits. He wanted to reach out and help this young friend avoid the pitfalls that befall free spirits. From deep inside, he began to feel the need to express his feelings in a poem. One day the poem came:

FREE SPIRIT

Who are you?
Where does your joy come from?
Where do you get your energy?
Why are you so beautiful?
Why is the world so frightened of you?
How do you protect yourself?
And . . . Where do you go?

Answers to all these and more
I want to know
But, above all,
Why do I love you so?

As the man finished the words, he found the answer to the puzzle. He wasn't writing those words about his young friend, he was writing them about himself! He was writing about his own free spirit—a part of him that life had taught him to distrust, a part of himself that he had powerfully repressed. The poem was a message from his feeling function that he could no longer crush such an important part of himself. He needed to allow himself to be the free spirit that he was. He also needed to be aware of when it was appropriate and safe to be a free spirit and when it was not.

It is important to distinguish, then, when we are consciously using our inferior function and when it is in control of us. When the inferior function controls us, it is important to understand whether it is our enemy or our friend. If it is serving as our friend, then we may need to stay with it for a while to learn its lessons for us. For when we learn its lessons, it will go away! If it is serving us ill, then there are some things we can try to do to re-establish ourselves in control. One of them is to ask ourselves questions out of our dominant function. Thus:

- If inferior sensing is in control, try to refocus energy on what the possibilities are.

- If inferior intuition is in control, ask what the facts are.

- If inferior thinking is in control, ask what matters right now.

- If inferior feeling is in control, ask what logic suggests.

In each of the sixteen type descriptions in the second chapter, there are passages that describe how the inferior function is likely to manifest itself. The descriptions are not horoscopes, nor were they written exclusively by observing the behavior of each of the types. They draw heavily on Jung's insights into the dynamic interaction of the functions.

What about the other less developed function? Experts have given it so little attention that even its name suffers. It is called, simply, the third function. Some have tried to dress it up a little by calling it the tertiary function, as if the Latin word for "third" helps!

The third function is, of course, the opposite of our auxiliary function. Thus:

- If sensing is the auxiliary function, then intuition is the third function.

- If intuition is the auxiliary function, then sensing is the third function.

- If thinking is the auxiliary function, then feeling is the third function.

- If feeling is the auxiliary function, then thinking is the third function.

What can we say about the third function? Unlike the inferior function, we have more conscious control over it than we do over the inferior. Like the inferior function, we can often make effective use of it when we need to, provided that we are patient with it and ourselves. As with the inferior function, we are awkward and make mistakes when using it.

Often, an important key to our ability to do things that call for third function skills is to establish favorable conditions for it. This includes recognizing that our third function is extraverted if our auxiliary is introverted or introverted if our auxiliary is extraverted.

Those whose third function is extraverted generally make more effective use of it if they use it when they are with others. Those whose third function is introverted do better if they do third function activities when alone. Many people find that with perseverance they reach a point when using the third function provides them with a sense of accomplishment and pleasure.

X   How Do We Know Which Function Is Which?

WARNING, WARNING, WARNING: This will not be an easy section. It cannot be casually read through and easily understood. And yet, for those who want to make the fullest use of type, it is important to master the guidelines for identifying how the parts combine. Ideally, one should see or hear the four initials of a type and be able to say: "Oh, yes. These are the extraverted and introverted functions. These are the dominant, auxiliary, third and inferior functions."

Soon after I was introduced to type years ago, I began to realize how important it was to know how to identify which function is which. There was very little written on the subject. I read the material that was then available over and over again. Then I set out to test my knowledge. I wrote out the initials of the sixteen types. I went over each one and, with what seemed angonizing slowness, labeled each function.

If you really want the most complete understanding of type, you, too, may want to work through this section with paper and pencil. As you read the guidelines and examples, write down the initials of other types. Apply the guidelines and see what you come up with. Check your answers out by turning to the attitude and function descriptions in the early part of this book.

Overview:

Guideline 1:

Js extravert their judging function, T or F.
Js introvert their perceiving function, S or N.

Ps extravert their perceiving function, S or N.
Ps introvert their judging function, T or F.

Let's try to illustrate, using lower case "e" to signify the extraverted function, and "i" to point to the introverted function. Here's what it looks like with an ENTJ and an INTP:

	E			I
i	N		e	N
e	T		i	T
	J			P

Guideline 2:

Es: The extraverted function is dominant.
      The introverted function is auxiliary.

Is: The introverted function is dominant.
      The extraverted function is auxiliary.

Let's stay with our ENTJ and INTP examples and now try to illustrate which function is dominant and which is auxiliary:

	E			I	
i	N	auxiliary	e	N	auxiliary
e	T	dominant	i	T	dominant
	J			P	

Guideline 3

The opposite of our dominant is inferior.
It is introverted if the dominant is extraverted.
It is extraverted if the dominant is introverted.

The opposite of our auxiliary is our third function.
It is introverted if the auxiliary is extraverted.
It is extraverted if the auxiliary is introverted.

(Not all students of Jung agree with these last two statements. They say Jung believed that if the dominant is extraverted then the other three functions are introverted, and vice versa. It just doesn't seem to work that way.)

Using our ENTJ and INTP examples, the four functions relate like this:

Type	Less Developed Functions
E	
i N auxiliary	e S third
e T dominant	i F inferior
J	

I	
e N auxiliary	i S third
i T dominant	e F inferior
P	

The rationale behind the first guideline

Why do judging types extravert thinking or feeling?

Judging types want their external worlds organized. They want things settled. They look at the world and see decisions that need to be made. The preferences that enable them to organize their external worlds are the judging functions, thinking or feeling. Thus judging types extravert T or F, whichever is their preference. That's why in some ways it is true that J really doesn't stand alone. It goes with T or F. There are TJs and FJs. The other functions follow a rule of opposites. Thus:

If the preferred judging function is extraverted, then the preferred perceiving function (sensing or intuition) is introverted. In an important way, the two preferred functions do not compete with each other. One is supreme in the external world, the other in the internal world.

The less well developed judging function is introverted.

The less well developed perceiving function is extraverted.

EXAMPLE: ENTJ. The J means that:

T is extraverted. Using the rule of opposites:

N is introverted.
F is introverted.
S is extraverted.

Why do perceiving types extravert either sensing or intuition?

Perceiving types want their external worlds to allow them to be flexible. They want to be free to pursue information and understanding. The functions that allow them to do that are the perceiving preferences, sensing or intuition. Thus, perceiving types extravert their preferred perceiving function, S or N. Again, in this sense, P really doesn't stand alone. There are SPs and NPs. Again, the rule of opposites tells us about the other preferences:

If the preferred perceiving function is extraverted, then the preferred judging (T or F) is introverted.

The less well developed perceiving function is introverted.

The less well developed judging function is extraverted.

EXAMPLE: INTP. The P means that:

N is extraverted. And the rule of opposites says:

T is introverted.
S is introverted.
F is extraverted.

The rationale behind the second guideline

Extraverts and the dominant function:

The outside world is more important to extraverts than is the introverted world. They deal with the extraverted world, therefore, through the strongest part of themselves. That's the dominant function. And that is why extraverts extravert their dominant function. The rest follow in order.

The other preferred function is the introverted auxiliary.

The opposite of the dominant becomes the introverted inferior function.

The opposite of the auxiliary becomes the extraverted third function.

EXAMPLE: ENTJ. We know by looking at the middle letters that ENTJs prefer intuition over sensing, thinking over feeling. We have already seen that for ENTJs thinking is extraverted and intuition is introverted. Thus:

Thinking is both extraverted and dominant.

Intuition is both introverted and auxiliary.

The less well developed functions are sensing and feeling. Therefore:

Sensing is the extraverted third function.

Feeling is the introverted inferior function.

Introverts and the dominant function:

For introverts, the inner world is more important than the external world. They prefer to use the strongest part of their personalities in that inner world. For that reason, their dominant function is introverted. That is why, by the way, introverts can surprise people. When they get to know someone well or when something very important comes up, they may choose to share their more important inner thoughts. Again, the rest follow in order.

When the introverted function is dominant, it follows that:

The other preferred function is the extraverted auxiliary.

The opposite of the interverted dominant becomes the extraverted inferior function.

The opposite of the intraverted auxiliary is the introverted third function.

EXAMPLE: INTP. Again, we know by looking at the middle letters that INTPs prefer intuition over sensing, thinking over feeling. Continuing with the INTP example above:

Thinking is both introverted and dominant.

Intuition is both extraverted and auxiliary.

The less well developed functions are sensing and feeling. Therefore:

Sensing is the introverted third function.

Feeling is the extraverted inferior function.

Notice that for both ENTJ and the INTP, the dominant, auxiliary, third and inferior functions are the same. But also notice that the types exactly reverse which functions are extraverted and which are introverted. That fact makes them very different personalities. Read their descriptions and see!

XI The Importance of Balance

Each type, as Myers so aptly put it, "has its own paths to excellence and pitfalls to be avoided." Type balance helps us to make the most effective use of our strengths and avoid our weaknesses. What does "type balance" mean? For extraverts, it means having a well developed introverted side. For introverts, it means having a well developed extraverted side.

Why? Because a balance of extraversion and introversion helps each type make effective use of both perception and judgment. Perception without judgment, as we have seen, produces fickle and undependable personalities. Judgment without perception leads to another kind of imbalance— rigidity. Balance, then, is an important part of what we call "good type development." It includes the following:

1. Our preferences are clear

2. Our dominant function is clearly in charge of our personality. The auxiliary is strong and subordinate. Both work together as an effective team.

3. We maintain a balance between extraversion and introversion.

4. We make use of those functions that are less well developed when the situation calls for it.

5. When our preferences are not clear, we suffer confusion or conflict.

For example:

- A man whose preference with regard to extraversion/introversion wasn't clear felt restless when alone. He was ill-at-ease when with people he did not know. He did not make effective use of his time alone. Neither was he as effective as he would like when with others.

- An I-FJ had trouble sorting out her preference with regard to sensing and intuition. She retreated into almost total silence when with people she did not know well. She said little even to those she did know well. One of these preferences was her dominant function, the other her inferior. She was unable to sort out her important inner world and therefore lacked that sense of security she needed to feel comfortable with others.

- An IN-P was confused with regard to his thinking/feeling preference. Making decisions of any importance was agony to him. He frequently ran away from facing decisions by going surfing!

- A woman whose preference for judging or perceiving was unclear berated herself for not being a manager. The judging part of her pushed her in that direction. She would begin to search for managerial positions and then fail to follow through on her initial explorations. The judging/perceiving conflict created an unhappy stalemate.

What can be done when a preference is unclear? What to do is not always clear and may not be easy. Often what helps is to try to be aware when we are using which preference. In the first example, the man whose preference on extraversion/introversion was unclear began to pay close attention to himself when in extraverted and introverted situations. He realized that he pushed himself into many of his extraverted activities. He really did not enjoy them as much as he did his introverted time. He found introverted things energizing, extraverted activities draining. Given insights like these, he became more comfortable with himself as an introvert. He stopped driving himself to be what he was not.

A close friend told the IN-P that his judging preference was feeling. The friend suggested that the IN-P ought to listen to himself when he was trying to make a decision. Was he having difficulty because logic couldn't see a clear answer? Or was it because the situations he was attempting to resolve triggered several different values, each of which led in different directions? Was it neither? Was the real difficulty that thinking and feeling were arguing with each other inside his mind?

It turned out to be the latter. Having figured that out, his friend suggested that he try to listen to his value decisions and act on them. When he did so, he became comfortable that feeling was his preferred judging function. He no longer attempted to escape from difficult decisions in his life.

These, however, are success stories. Life is not always so simple as that. It often takes time, patience, experiencing life—and help—to sort things out. Jung believed, and it seems to fit experience, that we are born with a predisposition toward one type. Life is an unfolding of how effective we are going to be in our type. That's a big challenge!

An extraverted-introverted balance remains one of the most important keys to good type development. There is no extravert who does not have an introverted side, nor is there an introvert who does not experience some extraverted needs. Extraverts need less introverted time than introverts, and introverts need less extraverted contact than extraverts. But both need a balance.

Why? Because of the relationship between extraversion/introversion and the functions. More specifically:

- Judging types make use of their preferred judging function, thinking or feeling, when they do extraverted things. If they limit their extraverted activities, they will not make good judgments. If, on the other hand, they spend too much time with others their judgments will lack good data.

  When alone they make the most effective use of their preferred perceiving function, sensing or intuition. Thus, judging types who spend too much time in the extraverted world are likely to make judgments based on inadequate data. We've all seen people like that. For them was the slogan made: "My mind is made up, don't confuse me with the facts!"

  EJs starve their auxiliary function, which is where their best data comes from unless they provide themselves with some time alone. IJs starve their dominant function unless they protect their time alone.

- Perceiving types, in turn, need time alone if they are to make their best judgments. Those perceiving types who give themselves little time alone become fickle and undependable. They follow the whim of the moment—the perfect flakes!

  EPs who spend little time alone starve their auxiliary function, which is their best source of good decisions. IPs who do not protect their introverted time starve their dominant function. At best, they operate from the second-best part of themselves.

It would be difficult to overestimate the effect of balance between extraversion and introversion in our lives:

- Am I a judging type? Do I see myself as getting into trouble because I am rigid? Are my decisions working for me or do they often turn out to get me into trouble? Have I organized all the spontaneity out of my life? Do I feel like I'm a little brittle, like I could break if someone pushed me too hard. Do I have to put up this thick wall of judgments between me and others and constantly defend them? If so, what are the chances that I spend most of my time with others, that I spend very little time alone? If that's true, there may be a simple solution. Seek time alone and concentrate on what kind of information seems to come up. Can I develop enough discipline to ask people for a little time to think something over and then get back to them? When alone, I will see information that I might otherwise have overlooked. When I do return to the discussion, I will bring a more balanced perspective to my judgments.

  On the other hand, as a judging type if I need to make decisions, I should not do that alone. I'll do that better if I am with others, sharing my judgments, listening to their reactions, shaping and revising my decisions as seems appropriate. Alone, making judgments is difficult and frustrating. Let me do that work, then, with others.

- Am I a perceiving type? Do I find that I am having trouble making decisions? Am I more disorganized than I would like to be? Do I seem to be moving from one project to another, never really completing satisfactorily any one of them? Am I always having to pull "rabbits out of hats" because I put things off to the last minute? If so, then what are the chances that I do not spend enough time alone? If so, the answer is relatively simple. Structure my life so that I have to spend more time alone! If I do, I will achieve some of the stability that I seek. Why? I don't do well making decisions when I am in extraverted situations.

On the other hand, as a perceiving type, if I want to explore information, I will be frustrated if I try to do it when I am alone. I get my best information by being with others. In my talking things over with others, all kinds of information emerges. So, if I am solving a problem and I get stuck, what should I do? Talk to others! That's my best way of getting unstuck.

Knowing, then, which of our functions is extraverted and which is introverted can help us make wise decisions about how to manage ourselves. It can help us to be the most effective we can be. Whether we are extraverts or introverts, we need to achieve a useful balance between extraversion and introversion. It is a critical part of good type development.

XII   The Developmental Process and Type Development

One of the early pioneers in the uses of psychological type is W. Harold Grant. He suggests that Jung believed there was a developmental process with regard to type. That process, for most of us, has the following stages:

- From birth to about six, we use all four functions in an undifferentiated way. There seems no pattern to it. It's as if we are testing the functions to learn which will serve us best. Even when from close observation a child's type seems clear, there is a great deal of experimentation.

- From six until about twelve years of age, the dominant function begins to assert itself as the one in charge of the personality.

- From twelve until twenty, the auxiliary function emerges as a powerful support to the dominant. The "power team" of our personalities takes shape. These are adolescent years, which Erik Erikson has called the identity formation period of life. Is it possible that those who experience "identity crises" in adolescence may not be clear as to what their type preferences are?

Myers conducted a study of high school students with high IQs but poorly developed auxiliary functions. She found that they did not often live up to their academic potential. Then she compared their academic performance with students whose IQs were in a "normal" range but whose auxiliary functions were clear. She found that the latter performed academically above the norm for their academic ability. The tentative conclusion she drew was that with good type development students can make the most of the abilities they do have. Those with IQs in the gifted range, however, are not likely to be able to overcome poor type development.

- From twenty until about thirty-five, we find ourselves making room in our lives for our third function. We begin to be able to make more effective use of our third function during these years. We may even become involved in activities or hobbies that require the use of that function.

- From thirty-five until about fifty, our inferior function demands our attention. Is it possible, then, that what has been called our "mid-life crisis" is type related? Would research indicate that those who share the same inferior function have similar "mid-life crises"? There is a real possibility that this is so.

- From fifty on, we have available to us all four functions. Now, however, we use them in a differentiated way as opposed to the undisciplined, undifferentiated way of early childhood. That is, we can use each function as different situations require us to do so. We continue to depend most on our dominant function. The auxiliary function continues to be the most loyal and effective subordinate to the dominant. We still need to be patient and forgiving with the third function, but we use it more with less difficulty. Finally, though the inferior function remains for the most part out of our conscious control it does not act in such a rambunctious fashion. We have allowed it a place in our lives, and that takes some of the pressure off of it. We also have a better understanding of it. We listen to it more wisely. We defuse it more quickly. We may even provide a healthy release for its energies in hobbies or other leisure time activities.

Think of a four passenger car driving over often strange and unfamiliar roads. Obviously it must have a driver, someone in charge. That's the dominant function. The car cannot function without one. The auxiliary function is in the front passenger seat. Clearly, it's very helpful in this journey through life to have a helpful companion there. The auxiliary looks out for whatever the dominant does not pay attention to. In the back seat, right behind the driver is the inferior function. Behind the front-seat passenger is the third function.

When we are in our twenties and thirties, if we are married and have two young children, think what it's like taking a long, tiring trip.

"Mommy, when are we going to get there?"

"Daddy, I have to go to the bathroom!"

"Mommy, he hit me!"

Much as we love them, they can make the drive a difficult one.

Now, move into our late thirties and forties. The children are older. They amuse themselves for long periods of time. The family can even have some good conversations. And if we parents want to do some sightseeing along the way, the children may even enjoy the experience. The drive is an easier one.

And so it is with type.

XIII   Putting Type Theory To Work

The keys to making effective use of type theory are simple. Know it and use it. Using it means learning to look at one's own behavior and the behavior of others through the perspective of type. That includes, in particular, taking into account how the parts combine. In the form of letters to friends, here are some examples of using type:

1. Dear Pat: You and I have talked a lot about how you get into trouble. I've noticed particularly that you start off every school year, every new part-time job, every project, with the best of intentions. Unfortunately, for you good intentions are about as far as it gets. After a short while, the school work suffers, you become less than dependable on your job, and you don't follow through on your projects.

   You've talked with me about it and asked what's going on and what you can do. I can give you a suggestion. You are an ENTP. That means that intuition is your best developed function— your dominant function—and that it is extraverted. In simpler terms, the ideas you get from your intuition are what excite you the most. You get in touch with that part of yourself most powerfully when with others. Thinking is your auxiliary function and it is introverted. That means that you are likely to look more critically at your ideas and form sound judgments about them when you are alone. Got the picture, Pat?

   OK, now, what have I noticed about you? You spend almost no time alone. When you lived in my house, I frequently watched you get up in the morning. You almost always stopped on the way to the bathroom to pick up the phone. You just had to find out where the action was. You had to know who was doing what that day!

   If you want to do better, I have a simple suggestion. Spend more time alone. Do you think you could discipline yourself to do that? I'll bet if you did, you'd find that you begin to follow through on your good intentions! Try it, Pat. Love, Alan

2. Dear Brad: For three summers now, Brad, you and I have talked about you and jobs. You are 27. You have a Master's degree in sports medicine. You were a trainer and an instructor at a college for a year. You took a fling at being an assistant golf pro. You went through the training to be an insurance salesman. You worked last winter in a variety of jobs including construction and selling memberships to a health club! You spend your summers on our island making money painting houses.

   You say you are increasingly unhappy at not being able to settle down in one career. You are almost afraid to admit that part of the problem is that you want some kind of work where you are the center of attention. You ask me if there is anything I can say that might be helpful. Well, let me try.

   First, Brad, I want to warn you—your parents are judging types as are your brother and sister. You grew up in a family where you were the only perceiving type. The most important woman in your life right now is also a judging type. It is possible that their influence on you makes you somehow think your life's path ought to be settled at 27?

   Brad, it is not uncommon for perceiving types to be asked all their lives by judging types: "Well, what are you going to do when you grow up." But perhaps that is not the answer. Let's look at it from another perspective:

   Brad, there are some patterns in your behavior that I began to notice this summer. First, you set goals that are extremely challenging. Often the goals seem out of touch with reality.

   Do you remember this summer when my son Tom visited us and the three of us set off for a five mile run? Tom began to pull away from us. Some friends of yours joked about it when you and I ran past them. You yelled out that you would be ahead of Tom when we came past that point on the way back.

   Now, let's look at that. You had no idea what kind of shape Tom was in. He had already disappeared out of sight on the road ahead, so you had no idea of how much ground you had to make up. Still, you set that goal of beating him. You could have had no idea if you could make it.

With that story in mind, let's look at your behavior pattern with regard to a career. There, too, you set high goals. Very soon you get discouraged, decide that you don't like what you are doing and then quit. Then the process starts all over again.

Brad, you are an ESTP. So, in terms of type theory, sensing is your dominant function and it is extraverted. Thinking is your auxiliary function and it is introverted. Feeling is your third function and intuition is inferior.

When I apply that knowledge to what I've seen you do, I can make out a case that you are setting your most important goals out of your inferior intuition. That, Brad, is your worst guide. It's likely only to lead you into trouble. Once in trouble, sensing sets in, if I can put it that way, and you recognize the specifics. The gap between reality and the goal is so great you get discouraged and you make a feeling judgment. "I don't like selling insurance." "I don't like being a trainer—it's a flunky's job."

Now, feeling is your third function. Although it doesn't cause you as much trouble as your intuition, it is not your best way to make judgments. In short, you seem to be operating out of your inferior and third functions, not your dominant and auxiliary.

What would I suggest? First, discuss your next job or career move with someone else. Focus hard on the realities. Be practical. Be specific. If you do, you'll be using your extraverted sensing, which is your type's great strength. Second, take some time alone to let your introverted thinking come into play. Review critically what you've come up with. Make your decision about what to do as logically and analytically as you can. Establish realistic criteria for how you will judge whether you have made a good move for yourself or not.

Don't be surprised if it takes a while to do these things. Don't be surprised if you get impatient and want to just move ahead—ESTPs are that way—but hang in there with it. See what happens. I hope this helps. Take care, Alan.

3. Dear Joanne: I notice that when you are discouraged and critical of yourself, you often come to me and, after telling me in detail what's going on, ask if you did the right thing. I try to be helpful, but almost never is what I say useful to you. If anything, you seem to get more upset and get more critical of yourself. You seem to ignore all the things I say that are positive. You are supersensitive in the way you pick up on all the things I say that may sound critical to you.

How I could have been so stupid all these years is beyond me. You are an ESFJ and I am an INTP. Thinking is your inferior function, and it is my dominant. I've always addressed your question out of my dominant thinking. Because thinking is your inferior function, you are naturally going to ignore all the supportive things I say. You look for all those statements that suggest that what you've done might logically have been done a little bit differently.

I'm not going to do that any more. I've learned my lesson. I've found out that I need to ignore your appeal to my logic (oh, my, is that difficult for me!). I need to shift the ground of the discussion back to your dominant feeling function. I've done that sometimes by saying: "Joanne, I can't deal with the question the way you've put it. In this situation, what is important to you, what matters to you?" We generally have much better discussions then.

Or I can say as I once did, "Joanne, if the only thing that mattered to you right now was to take care of yourself, what would you do?"

Remember what happened? You said without a moment's pause: "Oh, that's simple. I'd have a hot fudge sundae, go home, read a book and take a nap."

When I asked if there was any reason why you couldn't do that, your SJ sense of responsibility caused you to pause a moment, but you said, "No. What a great idea. Thanks."

It wasn't even my idea!

I now try to apply my knowledge of type to ask the right question. I share this with you in the hope that you, too, can help yourself when you are caught up in your inferior thinking. It will always tell you awful things about yourself. When that happens, try to look at yourself and the situation through your feeling judging side. It will give you much more supportive answers! Try it. You'll like the results. Love, Alan.

XIV How Type and Temperament Relate

Sooner or later, most people who become seriously interested in Jung's theory of type and Keirsey's theory of temperament begin to wonder about the relationship between type and temperament. In Jung's theory, the importance of the dominant function and its extraverted or introverted orientation cannot be overestimated. In fact, in his book, Psychological Type, he provided descriptions of eight, not sixteen, types. He gave the types names that were based on the dominant function and its orientation. Thus, for him the eight basic types were:

Extraverted sensing (ESTPs and ESFPs)
Introverted sensing (ISTJs and ISFJs)
Extraverted intuitive (ENTPs and ENFPs)
Introverted intuitive (INTJs and INFJs)
Extraverted thinking (ESTJs and ENTJs)
Introverted thinking (ISTPs and INTPs)
Extraverted feeling (ESFJs and ENFJs)
Introverted feeling (ISFPs and INFPs)

Jung's grouping of types is not consistent with Keirsey's temperament grouping of SJ, SP, NT, and NF. For example:

- Extraverted intuitives (ENTPs and ENFPs) belong to two different temperaments (NT and NF).

- Introverted intuitives (INTJs and INFJs) also belong to two different temperaments (NT and NF).

- Extraverted thinkers (ESTJs and ENTJs) belong to two different temperaments (SJ and NT).

- Introverted thinkers (ISTPs and INTPs) belong to two different temperaments (SPs and NTs).

- Extraverted feeling types (ESFJs and ENFJs) belong to two different temperament groups (SJs and NFs).

- Introverted feeling types (ISFPs and INFPs) belong to two different temperament groups (SPs and NFs).

Only extraverted and introverted sensing types fit into the same temperament groups. Extraverted sensing types (ESTPs and ESFPs) fit into the SP temperament. Introverted sensing types (ISTJs and ISFJs) fit into the SJ temperament.

Are they as incompatible as they seem? Does one theory work and the other not? No. Just because the eight Jungian types don't fit neatly into the Keirsey temperament groupings does not mean that type and temperament are necessarily incompatible. Both theories provide rich insights into human behavior.

Using the yin-yang symbol from the ancient Chinese Tao helps to illustrate how the two theories can form part of a larger whole. The symbol looks like this:

The yin-yang symbol represents how things that seem incompatible form part of an ongoing flow of life's energy, and are in fact part of a cosmic whole. Thus, type and temperament pictured within the yin-yang symbol look like this:

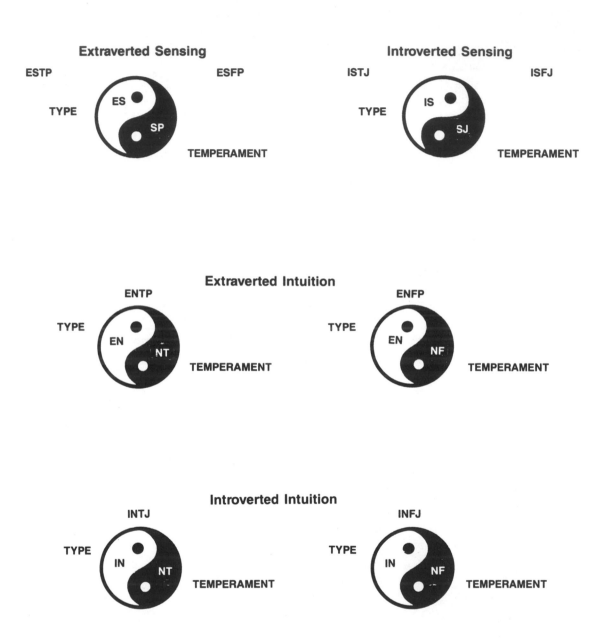

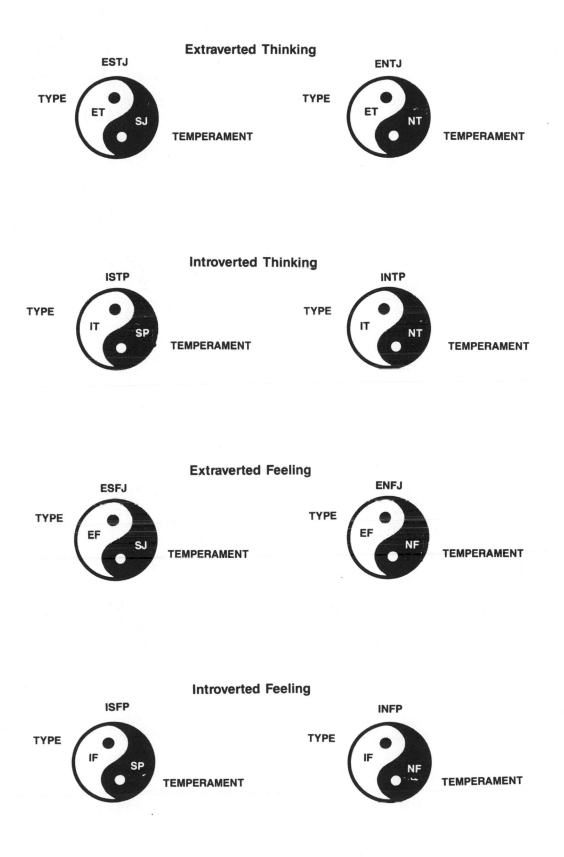

The yin-yang symbol helps to illustrate the idea of the continual ebb and flow of a personality between type and temperament. Thinking of foreground and background also helps. At times, type is in the foreground, and temperament recedes into the background. At other times, it's just the opposite. For example:

- When children approach their ESFJ mother to ask to do something unusual, they trigger her SJ temperament. It comes to the foreground. She bases her answer on two SJ questions: Is what they are asking safe? Is it within the rules? Often her answer is "no".

  If the children then get angry and try to push their mother into changing her mind, she stays frozen in her SJ temperament. Why? Because her authority is being questioned.

  If, however, the children appear to accept her answer and look disappointed, they trigger her extraverted feeling. When that comes to the foreground, she wants to please, to have harmony. If that happens, she works hard to find ways to compromise. She tries to figure out how they can do what they want and still meet her SJ concerns.

- An ISTP manager of a large city department responds to problems his mayor raises at a staff meeting as an SP. He wants to get out of the mayor's office to go back to his desk. He wants to call in his subordinates and do something—fast. He doesn't want to stay in the meeting with the mayor one minute longer than necessary.

  When taking a management development course, introverted thinking comes to the foreground. He attempts to figure out a conceptual relationship between a theory and some descriptive material based on that theory.

  Only if he can do so and see some practical value in it will he continue to pay attention in class. Otherwise, his SP temperament will take over. He will tune out—and probably walk out, too!

- An ENTJ corporate vice president for management development is an NT conceptualizer when he calls together a small group of consultants. He sees each of them as competent and experienced, and he wants to work with them to develop a new course in managing organizational change.

  As he does so, he may neglect his extraverted thinking responsibilities for a while as he enjoys the intellectual challenge. At some point in the sessions, his extraverted thinking nature asserts itself. He cuts off the discussion, makes command decisions, issues orders and acts on his decisions.

- An INFJ is an NF catalyst when as a gifted high school English teacher he plans and implements a new curriculum. His concern is to help students achieve their potential. He does not want them to sell themselves short in life. He wants to develop speaking and writing skills in students who are turned off by school and see no sense in a course like English.

  He moves into his introverted intuitive side when he sits in church and allows his inner intuition to take over. He sees rich religious symbolism in how the sun strikes the gold cross in the pulpit of a Congregational Church built in 1810. Later, he writes up his thoughts to share with others.

It is not necessary, then, as some would have us believe, to look upon Jung's type theory and Keirsey's temperament theory as incompatible. It is not necessary to accept one and reject the other. It is not useful to try to weigh the relative merits of one way of looking at human behavior over another. It makes much more sense—it pays rich dividends—to see both as providing different and useful insights into that unendingly rich mosaic of human personality.

Use It Or Lose It

For over fifteen years, type and temperament have been an important part of my life. During that time hardly a day has gone by without my using that knowledge. I never cease to be amazed at its staying power. I gain new and useful insights from it all the time.

During these past years, I have introduced many people to type and temperament. I've had two on-going disappointments: First, I've often been put in a position where I could do little more than introduce people to the four preferences, to temperament and to their descriptions. I know when that happens that people are cheated. They may find their exposure interesting and exciting. The chances of their being able to use the information effectively, however, are limited. The likelihood of their forgetting what they have learned is high. I hate to see that happen. If type and temperament turn out to be the latest in a long line of fads, it will not be because its potential is limited. It will be because those exposed to it have had an inadequate, superficial or inaccurate introduction. Tragically, there are too many people teaching type who don't know it themselves.

Second, many who are introduced to it don't make much effort to use it. They want to be given the insights. They don't want to find their own. The most effective presentation of type in the world is only an introduction. One must become one's own master. My stories are useful only as illustrations. You must create your own. Those are the ones that will make the learning worthwhile.

Using your knowledge means applying it to what you do. That, by the way, is an introverted task. Using it means also applying it to others. That's a more extraverted activity. We can all do both. I have found, however, that extraverts and introverts differ in their emphasis. Extraverts more quickly apply the knowledge to others. Introverts apply it more readily to themselves. Personally, I believe that it is safer and more appropriate to apply it first to understand oneself. I believe we are less likely to make mistakes, and we will learn more quickly from them. But that may be an introverted perspective.

Making effective use of type is a little like driving. There is a difference between wanting to learn how to drive and wanting to drive. Most of us see learning how to drive as a means to an end. What we really want is to be able to drive and to drive well. Why bother to learn how to drive if we have little or no intention of putting that skill to use? Type is like that. It is a skill that is of little or no value unless used. So, if you wish to retain and profit from what you've learned, use it!

Use It, Don't Abuse It

Knowledge is power. Power can be used or abused. There are those who react negatively to type and temperament because they are quick to see how it can be abused and blame the theory. Obviously, I don't subscribe to that view! That doesn't mean, however, that I do not carry around a healthy concern over the possibility that the knowledge will be put to questionable use.

I cringe when I remember one person whom I introduced to type. He held a very powerful management role, and he quickly became enthusiastic about type and temperament. He encouraged his staff and others whom he knew both in and out of work to take the Myers-Briggs Type Indicator. Not infrequently when he learned of the results, he'd call me and say: "I know so-and-so is such-and-such a type. Yet she came out as an -----. How could the instrument be so wrong?!" Based on only the scantiest of knowledge, he was absolutely confident that he could tell others' types.

Generally speaking, we abuse our knowledge when we use it to stereotype and limit others:

"Oh, she'll never make an accountant. Good accountants are ISTJs. She's an ENFP!"

"Don't bother to ask him. He's a sensing type. You're looking for new ideas."

I've heard statements like that more often than I'd like.

We also abuse our knowledge of type when we use it to excuse or justify our behavior:

"What can you expect. You know I don't pay attention to details!"

"I'm a thinking type. You cannot expect me to care about your feelings."

Justifying or excusing one's behavior constitutes an abuse of one's knowledge of type.

Katharine Briggs and Isabel Myers spent years trying to make Jung's theory of type readily available to us all. They believed that we should use that knowledge to be the best we can be and to enable us to understand and appreciate those who are different from us. We should use the knowledge they've given us, not abuse it.

And Finally . . .

As I've suggested, type and temperament have been an important part of my life for a long time now. I believe it has helped me as an individual, in relationships, as a parent, and at work. I believe it can do the same—perhaps more—for you. You are now at the end of this book, but, I hope, at the beginning of your own experience with type and temperament. May it be as rich and rewarding for you as it has been for me.